# The Forklifts
# Have Nothing To Do!

*Lead from the front*

*Joe Walter*
9/14/08

MARK
9:23

# The Forklifts
# Have Nothing To Do!

✦

## Lessons in Supply Chain Leadership

*Colonel Joseph L. Walden, CFPIM*

iUniverse, Inc.
New York  Lincoln  Shanghai

# The Forklifts Have Nothing To Do!
## Lessons in Supply Chain Leadership

iUniverse, Inc.

For information address:
iUniverse, Inc.
2021 Pine Lake Road, Suite 100
Lincoln, NE 68512
www.iuniverse.com

ISBN: 0-595-29496-0

Printed in the United States of America

This book is dedicated to my wife and my best friend, Kay, who has followed me around the world for over twenty-one years and my daughters, Amber and Bobbi, who have put up with my time away from home. It is also dedicated to the soldiers that I have worked with over the past twenty-five years that have been influential in teaching me the lessons captured in this book. I consider myself extremely blessed to have had the honor to work with some of the finest soldiers in the history of this nation.

All proceeds from the sale of this book will go to the Negro Leagues Baseball Museum in Kansas City, Missouri.

# *Contents*

# *Acknowledgements*

The first person that I need to acknowledge is my Dad, Thomas L. Walden, Sr. He inspired me to be the best I could be at what ever I did. His example of love and consideration for people helped to shape my leadership style and influenced how I treat people. Moreover, I knew he was behind me no matter what I did. I still carry a note he wrote when I was a High School wrestler—it is a bit yellowed and tattered but it reminds me, "win, lose, or draw I am for you." This note that has gotten me through some tough times over the thirty plus years since that note was written.

My Mother, Betty Walden, passed away while I was in college. Although she may be gone physically, her lessons in love and discipline remain as strong today as they were years ago.

Two young Captains took me under their wings when I first came in the Army and taught me how to be a logistician and a leader. Larry Matthews and Al Stein continue to mentor me twenty-five years later.

Charlie Ennis started out as a neighbor and mentor and turned into a great friend. When an Army bureaucratic error left me off a promotion list for several months, Charlie continued to have confidence in my abilities and capabilities. It was the support of friends such as Charlie and Beth Ennis that helped me get through that period personally and professionally.

Tom Edwards proved to be a friend and mentor. Mr. Edwards encouraged me to find out as much as possible about supply chains when I worked for him. He still encourages and inspires me to learn while providing guidance and support.

Harry Johnson started out as my boss when I was a Captain and then over time turned into a great friend and advisor.

"Uncle" Billy Pratt provides me with a sounding board for ideas and assistance in developing solutions. Thanks for getting me to and through Kuwait. However, most importantly thanks for your close friendship.

Melinda Woodhurst reminded me of the passion needed to be successful in this business and demonstrated the amazing power of leadership. Good friends are hard to find but are worth the effort to develop such friendships.

Last but not least, my staff, Charlie, Jeff, Mario, Lisa, Paul, Heather, Les, Christy, and Maria, for putting up with my antics and taking care of my family during my absence. You will never know how much I appreciate each of you.

# *Introduction*

It was December 17, 2002, and I was with the family taking a few days off in Laughlin, Nevada, when my cell phone rang at breakfast. My boss was calling to tell me that the rumors that I would deploy to Kuwait appeared to be true and that a by-name request was coming down through channels. A by-name request is usually considered an honor and not a tasking that one can get out of or substitute another soldier to do.

I had assumed that I was safe from this deployment since I was commanding a Non-deploying Brigade at the Army's National Training Center in the middle of the Mojave Desert. In addition, I had submitted the requisite paper work to retire from the Army in the summer of 2003 and had just received my approved "retirement" orders. Deploying and supporting the efforts in preparation for a potential war was not a problem but the timing for this deployment caught me completely off guard.

Upon my return to the office, just before Christmas, there was e-mail with a similar message from my assignments officer that a by-name tasking was being discussed. An "out of office" reply answered my message asking for additional information. The reply stated that the assignments officer was on vacation until the first of the year. Telephone calls to people "in the know" were greeted with the same message: there is a tasking coming but the details are not available until after the holidays.

On 2 January 2003, I received a telephone call from the Deputy Operations Officer for the National Training Center telling me that I was indeed tapped to go to Kuwait to operate the Distribution Management Center. The question was, "can you be there in three days? You have to be there in three days or you can wait up to three weeks." Since there were obligations as a commander to provide performance appraisals to all of my subordinates, I opted for the three-week delay. In addition, this would give me time to prepare the family and make sure that I received the necessary classified information briefings from the Intelligence Officer before deploying. Not to mention, I had to draw the proper equipment and uniforms, get the patches sewed on and pack my duffel bags for an uncertain period.

*The Forklifts Have Nothing to Do!* is about the lessons learned in supply chain management and leadership. It draws upon my experiences and my personal professional development program, as well as my experiences in Operation Iraqi Freedom.

*The Forklifts Have Nothing to Do!* The title for this book comes from an actual quote from a leader at the Theater Distribution Center in Kuwait that supported Operation Iraqi Freedom. I asked the leader why no one was working and his reply was "Sir, the forklifts have nothing to do." There was plenty for the forklifts to do in the Distribution Center at the time.

In the second chapter of *The Art of War*, Sun Tzu writes, "War is a matter of vital importance to the state; the province of life or death; the road to survival or ruin. It is mandatory that it be thoroughly studied." Few would argue that Supply Chain Management is a matter of vital importance to any company. It is indeed the road to survival or ruin. The biggest cause of failure for the dot.coms was a failure to establish a clear supply chain strategy. One major toy chain paid more in coupons to compensate for late deliveries at Christmas a couple of years ago than they made in profit. Truly, leaders of all companies must study supply chain management to ensure that the most efficient supply chain operations are in place and to posture their companies for survival and growth and not ruin.

What are matters of supply chain management? The matters of importance to supply chains and to corporations are those items that are of vital importance to the customers. It is imperative for survival of the company that these items are benchmarked internally and against the competition to ensure that you can provide the good or service better and faster than the customer desires and better than the competition. If what you are measuring is not important to the customer and to customer support, it should not be important to the company and therefore, should not be measured.

Is there a difference between supply chain operations in the military and supply chain operations in commercial industry? Yes and no, there are some significant differences and some very significant similarities. Both the commercial supply chain and the military supply chain have the same goal: get the right items to the right customer, in the right quantity, and at the right time to meet the needs of the customer. In the military, not meeting the needs of the customer could mean the loss of lives of soldiers. In commercial industry, not meeting the needs of the customers on a consistent basis could mean the death of the company.

*The Forklifts Have Nothing To Do!* will look at the similarities between military supply chain operations and those of commercial industry. These comparisons will enable the reader to apply the lessons learned in military supply chain operations to improving their own supply chains.

The chapter on leadership will set forth the difference between management and leadership. Although both are necessary for success, leadership is the essential ingredient to take your operations to the next level of excellence.

# 1

# *Operation Iraqi Freedom—Lessons Learned and Relearned*

○ ○ ○ ○ ○ ○ ○ ○ ○ ○ ○ ○ ○ ○ ○ ○ ○ ○ ○ ○ ○ ○ ○ ○ ○ ○ ○ ○ ○ ○ ○ ○ ○
*"I am certain that when the history of this campaign is written that people will look at this move that the land forces have made in this amount of time as being not only a great military accomplishment, but also an incredible logistics accomplishment."*

*—Lieutenant General John Abizaid,*
*Deputy Commander for Central Command*

1. The build up to Deployment

2. Processing through the Central Replacement Center

3. Arrival in Kuwait

4. Planning and Preparation

5. Developing the Theater Distribution Plan

6. Rock Drills—Rehearsal for the Real Thing

7. Pre-Combat Checks/Pre-Combat Inspections

8. Subsistence Support

9. General Supplies

10.  The Theater Distribution Center—History in the Making

Throughout history, armies have struggled to provide the right amount of supplies, in the right location, at the proper time. The early history of the US Army is punctuated by periods of dire need within the army. The winter at Valley Forge during the American Revolution is part of American lore as an example of the Army and General Washington's perseverance in the face of extreme military need. Until recently, efforts to avoid shortages in war have been directed towards establishing stockpiles of materiel and supplies across the combat zone, near the fighting force. Within the United States Army, this practice has become an unofficial policy known as "Just-in-Case" logistics. This style of logistics is an inventory management methodology that ensures supplies are available regardless of the cost or the need for an item of supply.

The practice of "Just-in-Case" logistics has produced excess inventories in every major deployment of soldiers since World War I. After the completion of Operation Desert Storm, there were more than 27,000 ISO containers on the ground. These containers were unopened and their contents were unknown. Additionally, there was more than two years of ammunition supplies stored, using the Days of Supply (DOS) computation, in the theater at the completion of the ground war.[1] The surplus in Desert Storm was similar to the waste during the Vietnam War two decades earlier.

During the initial deployment phase of Operation Joint Endeavor into Bosnia in 1996, "Just-in-Case" supplies created excess. Excess supplies surfaced again in support of Task Force Hawk's deployment into Albania in 1999. Within three weeks of arriving in Albania, Task Force Hawk's supply personnel started sending "excess" items back to Germany. An absence of a clear joint supply management concept may partially be the blame of some of these excess supplies. Part of the blame could be a lack of faith in the Department of Defense Supply Systems to provide the right item, in the right amount, to the right place, and at the right time.

The system is not the only reason for excess supplies. Logisticians have historically applied the "Just-in-Case" principle to ensure responsive, sustainable, and survivable Combat Service Support. "Just-in-Case" supplies help logisticians by creating a buffer that enables them to improvise logistic plans when faced with changes in operational plans and unforeseen mission requirements. "Just-in-Case" supply strategies also mask the inefficiencies in the supply system.

---

1.    Velocity Management Brief, http://www.cascom.army.mil/vm

# *The Build up to Deployment*

It was midnight on Thanksgiving Day 2002, the family and I had just gone to bed in Las Vegas, Nevada, after enjoying the first day off since early July. The cell phone rang. It was Colonel Billy Pratt calling from Kuwait to tell me that a by-name request was being prepared to have me come over to Kuwait and assist in setting up the Distribution Management Center to support potential future operations. There is nothing like the word "deployment" to wake you up from a sound sleep.

Another telephone call on Monday in the office provided more details on what I would be doing if I deployed. A lack of subsequent calls prompted me to believe I was off the hook and that I could continue planning for a summer 2003 retirement and the completion of my Brigade Command at Fort Irwin. Imagine the surprise when I got the call mentioned in the introduction almost three weeks later that I would most likely take off in January.

## *The Central Replacement Center*

Since I was not deploying with my unit, I was required to process through the Army's Central Replacement Center at Fort Benning, Georgia. This center does a phenomenal job of preparing a wide variety of personnel for deployments around the globe. My "class" consisted of soldiers of all ranks, sailors of all ranks, a couple of airmen, Department of Defense and Department of the Army Civilian employees, contractors, and employees of the Army/Air Force Exchange System. Some of the civilians had never put on a uniform or worn a protective mask. The cadre took great care in making sure they knew exactly how to wear the protective mask and made sure that everyone had confidence in the mask before allowing anyone to deploy.

The processing at the Central Replacement Center went smoothly because I had taken the time to get my equipment before leaving Fort Irwin. The replacement center expedited a number of us through the processes and we deployed after only three days of a normal seven-day process. An unexpected benefit of the time spent at Fort Benning was the relationships developed with other officers and Non-Commissioned Officers in that short period of time that became working relationships upon arrival in Kuwait.

## *Arrival in Kuwait*

After a thirty-three-hour journey that took me from Fort Benning to Atlanta to Baltimore to the Azores to Italy to Cyprus, I finally arrived in Kuwait. The good news was that my good friend Colonel Pratt was there to meet me at the plane. This precluded me from the four-hour ordeal of waiting for the baggage to be sorted and the subsequent bus ride to Camp Doha (North of Kuwait City). Remember the signs in the airport—"Check your bags, some bags look alike?" When three hundred soldiers with four duffel bags each get off an airplane, that sign is so true. Imagine over one thousand green duffel bags coming off the airport baggage claim carousel.

Since I was met at the plane, I was able to go straight to Camp Arifjan, the logistics headquarters for what was still called Operation Enduring Freedom. When I arrived at Camp Arifjan, the population of the camp was around 6,000 soldiers. By the time I departed two months later there were over 20,000 soldiers living in Camp Arifjan (about forty-five minutes south of Kuwait City).

## *Planning and Preparation*

*"The desert—a tactician's paradise, a quartermaster's nightmare."*

—*Attributed to a German General Officer*[2]

For the Warfighters, the buildup and preparation phase for combat operations can be a long and sometimes boring process. In fact, the papers quoted one soldier as saying the Operation should be called Operation Enduring Boredom because of the lack of things to do once the units moved into their base camps in the Kuwaiti Desert. For the logistician, this is a very intensive time of preparation and planning. Just like commercial industry, no logistician wants an operation to be unsuccessful because of the lack of logistics planning and preparation.

The planning for Operation Iraqi Freedom started over a year before the operation started. The early planning was purely contingency planning. With the immenseness of such an operation, to wait until the operation started would be foolish. The contingency planning included planning for what units would be necessary to meet the intent of the leadership. This phase of the planning had to consider what combat units would be necessary based on the planning assump-

---

2.    Thompson, Julian, Lifeblood of War—Logistics in Armed Conflict, Marston Book Services, Abingdon, England, 1991, p. 220.

tions. It also had to consider what logistics units would be necessary to support the combat units, what engineer units would be necessary to build base camps and repair the road networks, what civil affairs units would be necessary to conduct post hostility operations, and who would command such an organization.

Once it became evident that a combat operation would indeed be necessary to remove the Hussein Regime, it was time to put the right people in place to lead the operation. In his book, *Good to Great*, Jim Collins calls this "putting the right people in the right seats on the bus" before starting on a journey.[3] The staff for the Combined Forces Land Component Commander was hand picked based on their backgrounds and experiences. I had just been informed that I was selected as one of the "Top 20 Logistics Executives in America" and I had just completed the requirements for my APICS Certification in Production and Inventory Management (CPIM). There was no way I could argue that I was not qualified and still accept such an award and display the CPIM credentials. In addition, I had a good deal of experience with moving supplies in a desert environment based on my two assignments to the National Training Center in the Mojave Desert. Besides, this would be a graduation exercise for me to apply 24 years of experience.

The logistics staff was formed from the Third Army logistics staff and the staff of the 377th Theater Support Command, an Army Reserve logistics command based in New Orleans, Louisiana. The merger of the staffs of these two organizations created a single, functional logistics command and control center. The Transportation Command (the owner of all the transportation assets), the Movement Control Agency (responsible for controlling all transportation moves in the theater), the Engineer Command, the Distribution Management Center, the Personnel Command, and the Civil Affairs Command were all collocated with the 377th Theater Support Command. This decision placed all the functional support commands in the same location for ease of coordination and communication.

The predeployment planning phase included determining what supplies needed to be in Kuwait before the mass of soldiers started to arrive. A large amount of these supplies was already packed and on the Army's Prepositioned Ships. The preponderance of the supplies stocked in the General Supplies Distribution Center came from these ships. Detailed analysis matched the projected flow of personnel and supplies into the theater to ensure that the flow of supplies was sufficient to sustain the incoming personnel and build a contingency stockage to support potential operations if so directed. In doing so, the equivalent of

---

3.  Collins, Jim, *Good to Great*, HarperCollins Publishers, New York, 2001.

over 150 Wal-Mart superstores moved to Kuwait to support the projected 250,000 soldiers, sailors, airmen, and marines scheduled for deployment.

## Developing the Theater Distribution Plan

"What is a Theater Distribution Plan?" That was my first question in Kuwait when told that one of my responsibilities was to refine the plan and make sure it was sufficient to cover any contingencies based on the Contingency Plans. The first thing I had to do was find a copy of the Contingency Plan and quickly get up to speed on what could happen if the Contingency Plan was indeed converted to an Operation Plan. (For more on planning, see Chapter 4, Planning and Preparation).

Once I read the Contingency Plans (a couple of times to grasp the maneuver concepts that would need support), I started to search the Army's websites to find out what a Theater Distribution Plan was and what it should contain. According to Army Doctrine a Theater Distribution Plan is:

"…An appendix to the service support annex of the Army Forces service support plan. It explains the architecture of the theater distribution system and describes how to distribute units, materiel, equipment, and Combat Service Support (logistics and supply chain operations) resources within the theater through a series of overlays and descriptive narratives. It portrays the interface of automation and communications networks for gaining visibility of the theater distribution system and describes the controls for optimizing the capacity of the system. It depicts—and is continually updated—to reflect changes in infrastructure, support relationships, customer locations, and extensions to the distribution system. The distribution plan portrays a distribution pattern that is a complete Combat Service Support picture showing the locations of supply, maintenance, transportation, engineer (as appropriate), medical, finance, personnel, and field service activities. It becomes the tool by which planners and managers know where support flows and where it may be diverted as operational needs dictate."[4]

Armed with this information and a template of what a distribution plan should contain, I was ready to review what I found out was a two hundred page document. My first question to the staff was "Whom do you expect to read this?" Moreover, "What is the target audience?" Do not get me wrong, it was a great reference document but for the units in the field it was too big, too long, and too detailed. It contained annexes for every imaginable distribution in the the-

---

4.    US Army Field Manual 4-93.4, *Theater Support Command*, p. 5-9.

ater—there were annexes for personnel, mail, casualties, enemy prisoners of war, medical supplies, aviation supplies, movement control maps, and general supplies. Everything you ever wanted to know about distribution in Kuwait and Iraq was there.

The first task was to ensure that the distribution plan matched the latest changes to the Contingency Plan and then to create an abbreviated version that units could use as a quick reference. Upon completion of these tasks, we were ready for the next phase of the planning.

## *The Rock Drill*

The Rock Drill is a time honored military tradition.[5] The purpose of the drill is to rehearse all facets of an operation. During the operation of a rock drill, all possible contingencies are considered. A rock drill is a form of "war gaming" to ensure all options are considered for an operation. Contingencies covered in a rock drill could include all the actions that are necessary before an operation to ensure initial success. Such actions may include what supplies are needed and in

---

5.   A Rock Drill is conducted on a map board on the floor. The size of the theater and the size of the facility are the constraints on the size of the map board. A rock drill will usually look at several scenarios and phases in an operation. Traditionally, the senior commander present to set the stage and the conditions for the rock drill opens the rock drill. Included in the opening remarks are the commanders desired outcomes from the rock drill. The intelligence community then gives a presentation using the map board and markers on the board to show what the enemy is expected to do. (In commercial supply chains, this would most likely be the marketing personnel giving a presentation on how the competition will most likely react to the proposed project). The operations community then provides a detailed brief on what the friendly forces will be doing. Once the stage is set for the operation each commander will "drill down" to the details of what his/her units will be doing during that phase of the operation. Once a phase or contingency is completely covered, a follow on phase or contingency will follow the same sequence of events until the senior commander is satisfied that all phases and possible contingencies have been completely thought through and analyzed. This seemingly simple method of planning pays big dividends by allowing the participants to "walk the terrain" on the map board and visualize what is really happening at each interval of time during the operation.

   From a supply chain perspective, the goal of the rock drill is to identify all of the customers' requirements, identify any shortfalls in the support structure, and then wargame the potential ways to work around these constraints in order to meet the customers' needs.

what quantities to support the proposed concept. These actions could include what units needed to be ready to go before the start of the operation and what threats that would they face before starting the operation. Another possible contingency in the rock drill was how do you continue the support operations if the enemy interdicts the supply lines or destroys the fuel supply.

In commercial industry, the rock drill would be part of the business plan for a start up operation. In the case of a new product development, the rock drill would serve a useful purpose in determining all of the necessary options, customer responses, and competition responses. All of these responses would then shape the actions of the company and could possibly alter the original plan to ensure success.

For Operation Iraqi Freedom, we had multiple rock drills. From the supply chain perspective, there were three rock drills of significant interest. The first one of significant interest was the operational rock drill. During the rock drill every commander that would be involved in the combat operations stood on the warehouse sized map board spread across the floor and told his plan for the operations. At this time, everything was still contingent on the success or failure of the deterrence actions—but plans had to be in place if Iraq did not comply with the United Nations Resolutions. The plans and concepts of operation of the "warfighters" would dictate the necessary support from the logisticians. The purpose of this first major rock drill was to ensure that the actions of the coalition partners were coordinated and synchronized for optimum success. The United States Fifth Corps Commander and his subordinate commanders, the Commander of the United States First Marine Expeditionary Force, and the Commander of the British Corps briefed their requirements based on the published phases of the operation plan.

For the logisticians the importance of this first major rock drill fell into two major categories. The first was gathering a full understanding of the thought processes of the customers. The importance of this in military operations is just as important as it is in commercial industry. You have to know what your customer plans to do in order to know what he/she expects of you as a supplier. Understanding how the customer is thinking allows supply chain leaders to prepare a better forecast of future requirements and needs.

The second essential importance of this rock drill was that it allowed the key logisticians to hear first hand from the customer units what they were planning. The supported units expressed what they expected in the way of support to be successful and when they wanted it. As with any supply chain endeavor, knowing what the customer wants and when they want it allowed us to plan what we had to have on hand at what time to be able to meet the customers' needs.

The next two important rock drills for the logistics community focused solely on logistics functions. The first logistics rock drill focused on theater level distribution functions in support of the Combined Land Force Component Commander's intent for the operation. This rock drill was a two-day event. On the first day, all of the participants took the morning to become familiar with the terrain model on the floor and to do individual rehearsals. In the afternoon, a formal rehearsal was conducted for each of the scenarios that the commander wanted to cover. The sole purpose of this rock drill was to demonstrate to the war fighting commanders that their plans (as detailed in the first rock drill) had been carefully analyzed and the logistics plans were in place to cover any contingency that may branch out of their plans. Whereas the first major rock drill had the operational commanders briefing their plans, this rock drill had the logistics community briefing how they would support the operational commanders during the major phases of the potential combat operations.

The second rock drill took place four days later and the audience was the logistics community. The purpose of this rock drill was to refine the plans from the first rock drill and war game within the logistics community all potential contingencies. In addition, the logistics community used this rock drill as an opportunity to do some professional development instruction for our junior leaders to make sure they were fully prepared and understood their role in the overall operation. Like the first logistics rock drill, this one was also two days and used the same format and scenarios to refine the concepts of support for every commodity of supply and every possible form or support. We covered personnel, medical, military police, engineer support, route security, convoy planning, and what assets were available at what point in time to make these plans work. Leaders discussed what support was not available, what was the impact, and how we could work around that short fall.

The result of the rock drills was identification of those areas that needed immediate work to refine the support plan for potential operations. Another benefit of the rock drills was the interaction between the important players. The rock drill served as a forcing function for all supported elements within the logistics community to get their support requirements refined and updated based on some minor changes to the contingency plans.

Upon the completion of each rock drill, we conducted a mini-After Action Review to improve the conduct of future rock drills and to make sure that we captured all substantive comments. Once the After Action Review was completed, a copy of the comments and recommendations were compiled and forwarded to all interested parties. This served a secondary function of ensuring that all lessons learned and all directives passed out during the rock drill were acknowledged and understood by everyone in attendance. The more confusion that can be eliminated during the rehearsal, the better the chance of survival on the battlefield and the greater the probability of success of the operation.

## PreCombat Checks and PreCombat Inspections

Critical to success in combat, as well as in supply chain operations, is the concept of PreCombat Checks and PreCombat Inspections. For the military, this is nothing more than going through checklist of what is required to be with the soldier and what is required to be with a unit or piece of equipment. The PreCombat Check is analogous to the preflight check that a pilot goes through before every flight. The PreCombat Check/Inspection is the leaders' way of making sure that everyone is ready and has the proper equipment and preparation for the upcoming operation.

PreCombat Checks/Inspections include crew level drills for contingencies such as vehicle rollovers. Practicing these drills before actual operations ensures that everyone in the vehicle knows what to do if their vehicle rolls over. The same precautions are taken for vehicle fires to ensure personnel accountability and adequate preparation.

Sun Tzu tells us "One who is confused in purpose cannot respond to his enemy." Just as the rock drill prepares leaders and planners for any contingency, the PreCombat Checks and PreCombat Inspections ensure that individual soldiers are prepared for any contingency. An added benefit of these checks and rehearsals is a boost in confidence for the individuals.

In Supply Chain operations, the PreCombat Check is just as important as it is for the soldier. Leaders have to check their people to make sure that they are ready for the missions of the company.

## Subsistence Support to Operation Iraqi Freedom

"I can live without repair parts, I can live without fuel, but if I run out of food and water the war stops!" This came directly from a logistics general before the start of Operation Iraqi Freedom. This particular officer did not want to hear what we were doing to assist him in getting food and water forward or that his command returned ten trucks of unneeded rations that morning. He was more concerned with making a point and doing so in a rather rude manner in front of a room full of soldiers that had nothing to do with the distribution of food and water. Contrast this statement to the one made by Lieutenant General Walker, Commander of the US Eighth Army during the Korean War, "You can live without food, but you cannot last long without ammunition."[6]

Regardless of the manner of the conversation, there is some truth to the statement. Sun Tzu spoke of the need for rations twenty five hundred years ago. Frederick the Great mastered the supply of food for his soldiers and their animals more than two thousand years ago. Moreover, the crusaders in the eleventh century found out the hard way that food is a critical commodity for soldiers in combat.

Obviously, in a 400-kilometer run across desert terrain, repair parts and fuel are necessary to be successful. However, as was seen several times on CNN and Fox News, the distribution of food and water was critical to the morale of the soldiers and was important to the success of the operation. The old adage "an Army moves on its stomach" was definitely true during this operation.

The distribution of food and water was not one of the most successful operations during Operation Iraqi Freedom. In fact, the weakest link in the supply chain was the food and water distribution.

The distribution of water was complicated by the fact that a safe source of water was necessary for the production of drinkable (potable) water for the soldiers and marines using the Reverse Osmosis Water Purification Units (ROWPU for short). Because of the uncertainty of potential chemical contamination, the preferred method of distributing all drinking water was bottled water. The maneuver units did deploy forward with potable water in their soft fabric 3000-gallon truck mounted tanks and in their water trailers. However, in spite of this the majority of the drinking water came from bottled water distribution.

The providers of the bottled water were not prepared to ship the cases of water with sufficient plastic wrap to prevent the loss of bottles in transit. In fact, the bottles strewn on the side of the road between the Theater Distribution Center and the forces in Iraq looked a little like the breadcrumbs of Hansel and Gretel in the Grimm Brothers classic. The distribution of the bottled water lasted longer than expected due to the rapid movement of the military through the desert and the lack of a certified "safe" source of water for the water purification units.

---

6.    Appleman, R.E., South to the Naktong, North to the Yalu/The United States in the Korean War, Office of the Chief of Military History, Department of the Army, Washington, DC, 1961, p.182.

Food distribution was equally as complicated. Since the maneuver units did not pause in their move to Baghdad, the soldiers depended on Meals Ready to Eat (MREs, also known as "Meals Rejected by Everyone") and goodies from home.

One soldier told me that they went six days without a ration delivery and if were not for the goodies from home and the snacks that the soldiers brought with them, they would have gone hungry. The break down in the ration deliveries was partially due to the long distances between the distribution centers collocated with the Kuwaiti Public Warehouse Corporation[7] and the units in Iraq. By the time, the Third Infantry Division reached Baghdad; the lines of the distribution system were more than 600 kilometers. Part of the problem was the interdiction of the road network by the Iraqi Paramilitary forces. Moreover, part of the problem was in the lack of dedicated lift assets to move the rations forward.

The planning for Operation Iraqi Freedom was partially predicated on the use of local national (Host Nation) support. This was a problem because the local national trucks were not allowed to cross the Kuwait-Iraq border. A contract was awarded to a prominent defense contractor under the Logistics Civilian Augmentation Program (LOGCAP). However, once the hostilities started and with attacks on the convoys in Iraq, these drivers refused to cross the border. This caused a quick revision of plans of what trucks delivered to what locations. The solution was that any convoy that was going past the Kuwaiti border had to be a military truck with all "local" deliveries in Kuwait accomplished with the local national trucks. This split of responsibilities created an additional movement control requirement and increased the need for military trucks in theater.

The lack of MREs in Kuwait complicated the distribution of rations forward to the maneuver units. The requirement to use constant emergency resupply of the rations from the United States, the prepositioned ships, and Qatar added to the distribution problems but provided another source of supply. A further complication came when some of the bottled water was suspected to be bad (later proved to be an inaccurate rumor after careful testing by the Army's Veterinarian Corps). Another concern came from suspected contamination of some of the

---

7.    The original location of the ration storage and distribution center was split between the Kuwaiti port of Shuwaykh for MREs and the Public Warehouse Company for all fresh rations. The collocations of both activities into one location at the Public Warehouse Company reduced some of the security problems at the port, made command, and control a much easier task. In addition, the movement to one location reduced the forklift requirements and reduced the multiple handling of the water and rations.

preposition ships MREs. This turned out to be outdated coffee creamer and not contaminated food.

## General Supplies

The General Supplies for Operation Iraqi Freedom included clothing, cots, and all types of packaged petroleum products (oil, anti-freeze, fog oil, etc.), uniforms, office supplies, and repair parts. The majority of the general supplies for the initial build up and the start of any major campaign in the Kuwait-Iraq Theater came to Kuwait on the prepositioned ships. These supplies formed the nucleus of the General Supplies distribution centers. These distribution centers included one for clothing, office supplies, construction materials, and the package petroleum products, one for repair parts for the ground equipment, and one for aviation repair parts. The initial push of these supplies arrived in twenty and forty foot containers.

At the end of Desert Shield/Desert Storm, there were 27,000 containers in Saudi Arabia with contents unknown for most of them. This led to discovery learning by opening each container to find out the contents. Unlike Operation Desert Shield/Desert Storm in 1991-1992, we had a good idea exactly what was in the containers that came off the prepositioned ships.

This time around, the Department of Defense did not want a repeat of the Desert Storm problems. To counter this, every container shipped to Kuwait came with an active Radio Frequency Identification Tag on the outside. A shipping manifest on the outside and inside of each container served as a redundant backup, just in case something happened to the Radio Frequency Tag.[8] In addition, every shipment of supplies from Germany and from the United States had an active Radio Frequency tag on the Air Force pallet.[9] The movement control teams assigned to the airport unloading ramps, the Theater Distribution Center, and the Convoy Support Centers were equipped with hand held interrogators.

---

8.  On a few occasions, the Radio Frequency tag was damaged by container handling equipment making the redundant manifest shipping lists a valuable redundancy.

9.  The Air Force uses a special pallet for loading of the cargo planes. These pallets, depending on the configuration and type of cargo, contain up to eight standard warehouse pallets. The goal of the shipments from the United States was to have each Air Force pallet configured for a single consignee. This would allow for quicker processing of the pallets through the distribution center and reduce the handling of the supplies.

These interrogators supplemented the fixed interrogators at every major node transfer point in the supply chain.

The use of the Radio Frequency tags and the interrogators throughout the supply chain provided consignees and supply chain managers with visibility from the time the items were packed at the major distribution centers in the United States until the ultimate consignee received the supplies. The ability to provide the consignee and the supply chain managers with this visibility significantly reduced the redundant reorders of supplies experienced during Desert Shield/ Desert Storm. A lack of visibility during previous operations resulted in continual ordering of the supplies until something was received. This lack of faith in the system produced a large amount of excess supplies. Knowing the status of the order provided a boost in the soldiers' confidence in the supply chain to meet their needs. This capability is not too unlike the ability of a consumer or business to track a shipment coming from a supplier via FedEx or UPS. One side benefit of the added supply chain visibility was the ability to see what was coming and then plan the workforce activities around the incoming shipments.

We did encounter a hiccup in the process in the early days of the Theater Distribution Center. The instructions to the temporary help that we used the first two weeks of operation were to make sure that we accounted for all of the Radio Frequency tags. The interpretation was, "take the tags off as soon as the Air Force pallets arrived in the Theater Distribution Center."

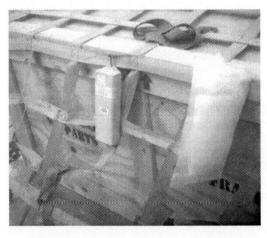

Figure 1. A Radio Frequency (RF) Tag attached to an Air Force 463L
pallet

Almost immediately, a new problem surfaced. The new problem was quickly brought to my attention. "My shipment arrived at the Theater Distribution Center but then the tracking stopped! Why? Where is my stuff?" When I walked the process to see why the tags were no longer active, I discovered that the soldiers were immediately taking the tags off the pallets and putting them in a box so they would not get lost. What I thought was clear guidance was not clearly understood. The standard practice when removing a tag is to reverse the battery when not in use to prolong the life of the tag. Of course, with the tag removed and the battery reversed, the active tag was no longer active and the data was no longer available.

The solution to this problem was actually a very easy one. A class for all of the soldiers working in the Theater Distribution Center emphasized the importance of the tag for customer visibility. Understanding this importance helped this problem to disappear.

## The Theater Distribution Center—History in Action

Never in the history of the United States Army has a Theater Distribution Center been established in an active wartime theater of operations.[10] There is a Theater Distribution Center in Kaiserslautern, Germany to support distribution operations for the United States Forces stationed in Europe. Previous operations used Theater Logistics Support Bases, but never formally established one central distribution center to support all the military forces in a theater.

The Theater Distribution Center for Operation Iraqi Freedom exceeded four million square feet, making it one of the largest if not the largest distribution center in the world. Collocated with the Theater Distribution Center was the distribution center for the general supplies, discussed previously.

The purpose of the Theater Distribution Center was to establish one central point for receipt and issue of all supplies coming into Kuwait for forces in Kuwait

---

10. The Department of Defense uses the term "theater of operations" to describe the geographic region that surrounds a conflict or potential conflict. Joint Publication 5-0, Doctrine for Planning Joint Operations, defines the theater of operations to be "a subarea within a theater of war defined by geographic combatant commander required to conduct or support specific combat operations. Theater of operations are usually of significant size, allowing for operations over extended periods of time." A theater of war is "defined by the National Command Authorities or the geographic combatant commander, the area of air, land, and water that is, or may become, directly involved in the conduct of the war."

and Iraq. The concept was for the Theater Distribution Center to function as a cross-docking[11] facility for supplies. Those supplies that came in dedicated for a specific unit were sorted and segregated at the Theater Distribution Center and placed in the unit's shipping lane or directly on an outbound truck. The Theater Distribution Center also served as the consolidation point for the supplies going to the different units from the general supplies distribution centers.

The Theater Distribution Center also served as the convoy consolidation point. Because of the threat to convoys during the hostility phase of Operation Iraqi Freedom, every convoy of trucks had to have armed escorts from the Military Police to protect the supplies and the personnel. Rather than send small convoys to the same location every day, we consolidated all convoys at the Theater Distribution Center and sent them forward as one large convoy consisting of all supplies, food, water, and personnel replacements.

How do you establish a Theater Distribution Center? What does it look like? The first day I went to the Theater Distribution Center this is what I inherited.

Figure 2. The Theater Distribution on Mar 10, 2003—day one of operations

11. The APICS Dictionary, 10th Edition, defines cross docking as: "The concept of packing products on the incoming shipments so they can be easily sorted at intermediate warehouses or for outgoing shipments based on final destinations. The items are carried from the incoming vehicle docking point to the out going vehicle docking point without being stored in inventory at the warehouse."

On first day I was there, the site was "wall to wall" pallets waiting to be sorted to customer locations and outbound delivery trucks. I was fortunate enough to have some excellent help to organize the distribution center into a functional center. Captain Nancy Sermons and Major Troy Kok worked diligently to get the center organized.

The first item of business was to clear the one thousand Air Force pallets[12] delivered over the first weekend of operations while processing the approximately four hundred pallets arriving daily. Establishing a flow for the distribution center that allowed for the least amount of handling of the supplies helped in this process and this set the stage for the eventual cross-docking operations. Since the yard was almost full on the first day of operations, this was a very important task. The final design allowed for the most efficient flow possible from the receiving area to the cross docking/customer lanes area. Every customer unit had a customer lane used to stage those items that we were not able to cross-dock to the outbound trucks.

At the same time that we were working on the flow of supplies through the distribution center, we had to do what the Army calls a "troop to task" analysis. Simply stated, what did we need in the way of personnel to make the distribution center function? Our initial estimate was based solely on what we thought would be the workload and the projected flow of supplies into the Theater.

Daily we were reminded that the Theater Distribution Center was the "Commander's Priority." Yet, daily for the first two weeks we had to operate with detailed personnel. These soldiers came from units whose equipment had not yet arrived or from units that only had part of their equipment in country and were not ready to assume their normal missions. New crews of soldiers every twelve-hour shift. Therefore, for every shift the first couple of hours were discovery learning as we instructed the soldiers on the distribution center functions. By the time we got a crew trained and working well, it was time to take them back on the busses and get a new crew.

The first order of business was to get forklifts to move the supplies. Since there were no additional supply units in Kuwait at the time, we had to contract with a local company to get "Third Country Nationals" and forklifts. This created a bit of a communication problem. However, even communications problems can be overcome through leadership.

The communications barrier resulted in a creative solution to marking supplies for customer bins. With all of the technology available today for distribution

---

12.   An Air Force pallet contains up to eight standard warehouse pallets of supplies.

operations and the tracking and routing of supplies, the simplest solution is often the best method. The simplest method in this case was to use spray paint to mark the pallets and containers for the units and then put large signs in front of the customer loading lanes. This allowed the forklift operators to match the pallets to the proper lane. This was a crude method but it proved to be the simplest solution to the communication problem. An added benefit was that it allowed for quicker identification of lanes for the soldiers when additional forklifts arrived for use in the distribution center. It also quickly identified visually what pallets and boxes were in the wrong locations before the loading operations commenced. The twenty-four hour operations coupled with the leadership of Captain Sermons and Major Kok enabled the detailed soldiers to transform the distribution center. Their efforts took the distribution center from the conditions in Figure 2 (shown here again for comparison) to the situation in Figure 3 in just over a week.

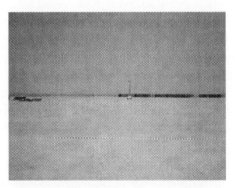

Figure 3. the Theater Distribution Center on March 18, 2003 looking back at the point the picture in Figure 2 was taken eight days earlier.

The third week of operations finally found us with a dedicated supply company to work in the distribution center. Along with the company came the leadership necessary to direct operations and additional forklifts and operators. The ability to use the same soldiers every day increased productivity and reduced the amount of errors. Luckily, this company was on the ground and operating before the hostilities started. At this same time, I received a full time assistant, Lieutenant Colonel Wayne Tisdale. Wayne proved to be a Godsend. His experience and work ethic made him a very valuable asset.

As stated earlier the distribution center design was to be a cross-docking facility. According to my daily journal of activities and observations, on March 27, 2003 (day eight of the hostilities) we were finally to the point that we were able to cross-dock the incoming supplies to the outgoing trucks. This was a major accomplishment. The same day more than one hundred outbound trucks left the distribution center in support of the forces in Iraq and those still in Kuwait.

There were days that the wind and sandstorms were so bad that visibility in the yard was less than ten feet. In addition, during the war there were days that operations were put on hold because of Scud Missiles launched in the direction of the command facilities nearby at Camp Doha. Throughout all of these disruptions, the soldiers and the "third country national" forklift operators operating the Theater Distribution Center performed in a manner that made me proud to be associated with them.

During the first week of operations I told people that the distribution center was like a Roach Motel, "Pallets checked in but the didn't check out." So it was a great relief when the cross docking started and the trucks started delivering supplies on a regular basis.

The Theater Distribution Center supported every US Army Division, the United States Marine Corps, the United States Air Force, the United States Navy (we even received parts for the USS Constellation that had to be flown out to the ship), the US Embassy, forces in Afghanistan, and the Army/Air Force Exchange System. The ability to have all supplies for everyone into one place simplified the tracking of supplies, allowed for consolidation of convoys going forward, and most importantly provided the customers with a single logistics point of contact for questions and supplies.

The first day of Operation Iraqi Freedom, we witnessed five Scud alerts requiring my soldiers to stop operations and put on their protective masks and protective chemical suits as a precaution. During the second alert, the Patriot Air Defense System actually fired missiles over our heads. This will get your heart pumping and the adrenaline flowing. It is amazing how fast you can put on a mask and protective suit when the missiles are flying overhead. The Patriots fired overhead five other times during the next two weeks. These situations only added to the drama and challenges of running the distribution center. However, the challenges of the distribution center were minor compared with the challenges of the soldiers moving through Iraq. Their needs are what kept the soldiers in the distribution center focused.

In combat, the factors are a bit different and the stress level is a bit higher than in everyday operations in a commercial supply chain. However, the need to focus on the need of the customer is just as important in commercial supply chain operations.

# 2

## *Achieving Supply Chain Excellence Through Leadership*

o o o o o o o o o o o o o o o o o o o o o o o o o o o o o o o o o

*"Leadership must be demonstrated, not announced."*

—Fran Tarkenton

"Sir, the forklifts have nothing to do!" Any one that has worked in a distribution center knows that there are times when the receipts and issues require more manpower than what is available and there are slower times when the "housekeeping" functions can be accomplished.

The Theater Distribution Center received an average of 100 trucks a day and on a good day shipped out more than 190 trucks of supplies a day. With a dedicated staff of less than forty soldiers and contract employees per shift, this was a daunting task and required leadership to keep the soldiers and the contract forklift operators motivated and focused.

On March 23, 2003, I arrived at the Distribution Center around 10:00 AM after the morning Battle Update Assessment to find no one working and all of the forklifts lined up in row. I found SSG Smith, the non-commissioned officer in charge of the day shift, and asked him why no one was working. Based on the forecasts for the day, we were scheduled to receive a larger than normal push of supplies to sustain the combat operations.

SSG Smith casually replied, "Sir, the forklifts have nothing to do!" I knew SSG Smith was referring to the fact that we had caught up and the receiving yard was empty, which is always a nice sight. Nevertheless, I also knew that there were many "housekeeping" functions to catch up on before the next convoy of trucks arrived with pallets coming from the airport.

We walked around the Distribution Center and looked at the piles of plastic from the Air Force pallets that needed to be in the trash bins. Then we walked through the customer lanes to look at the work required to prepare the lanes for the day's outbound shipments. A little mentoring and guidance was all he needed. SSG Smith agreed that the forklifts did indeed have something to do and organized the work details to accomplish them. His leadership ensured that the work was done and the soldiers understood the need to accomplish the tasks before the next wave of supplies arrived at the Distribution Center.

Over the past ten to fifteen years, large volumes of articles and books have been written about how to improve supply chains and supply chain management techniques. An even larger number of books published on management itself. In fact, a recent search of the Amazon.com website for "management" revealed thirty-two thousand titles on management. One of the most popular books of the 1980s was *The One Minute Manager*. In this chapter will look past managers and look at how to achieve excellence in your supply chain through quality leadership. The chapter looks at what true leadership is, leadership compared and contrasted to management, and applications of the leadership techniques to improve your supply chain and take it to the next level of excellence.

Leadership could easily be an acronym that lists the real virtues and qualities of a leader. This chapter addresses each of these virtues and qualities.

Using the virtues and qualities of leaders to form an acronym would look like this:

**L**oyalty
**E**thics
**A**ttitude
**D**evotion
**E**mployees
**R**espect
**S**upportive
**H**umor
**I**ntegrity
**P**rofessional Pride

Let us look at these values and qualities of a leader:

**Loyalty**. A true leader has to be loyal not only to those over him, but equally as important to those that work for him/her. General Patton once said, "I prefer a loyal staff officer to a brilliant one." Employees know when the leadership is loyal to them and concerned about their welfare and professional growth Loyalty from your employees is something that you must earn; you cannot buy loyalty. During the days of Sun Tzu (500 BC) and during the days of the Napoleonic Wars loyalty could be bought and sold. The problem with purchased loyalty is that someone else can purchase the loyalty just as easy. The free agent "wars" after the end of each professional sport season is a good example of purchasing loyalty—or better yet an example of loyalty only to the dollar. You cannot force loyalty on an individual nor can you buy it as you could during the Napoleonic days. The quick collapse of the Hussein Regime in Iraq is an example of the fickleness of "forced" loyalty. As soon as the forcing force is out of power, the "forced" loyalty will quickly evaporate and/or switch to another leader.

**Ethics.** There is no right way to do something that is wrong. Today's headlines are full of examples of unethical behavior by leaders of major corporations. Like integrity, once you have compromised your ethics, it is hard for employees to follow you. If something does not feel right, it probably is not right. Most world-class leaders have an ethical compass inside them. However, every so often, that compass goes out of whack and greed takes over. The Enron debacle is a good example of this.

A good way to measure the ethics of your actions—and remember it is your actions not your words that really shows the value of your ethics—is the *New York Times* Test. In an article in the *California Management Review*, Trevino, Hartman, and Brown explain this test, "When making a decision, ethical leaders should ask themselves whether they would like to see the action they are contemplating on tomorrow morning's front page."[1]

The real check of your ethics is not the ethics counselor at your company or the legal team for the corporation. The real check of your ethical behavior is the person looking back from the mirror. Growing up I found a poem in my Dad's desk drawer titled "The Man in the Glass." I later saw the same poem in Ken Blanchard and Dr. Norman Vincent Peale's book *The Power of Ethical Management*.[2] It is a powerful poem that basically says no matter what you accomplish in life and how successful you are if you cannot look yourself in the eye in the mirror you have failed. That is the true definition of ethical leadership. I have carried

---

1.    Trevino, Linda, Hartman, Laura and Brown, Michael, "Moral Person and Moral Manager: How Executives Develop A Reputation for Ethical Leadership," *California Management Review,* Volume 42, Number 4, Summer 2000.

2.    Blanchard, Ken and Peale, Norman Vincent, *The Power of Ethical Management,* Ballantine Books, New York, 1988, p. 45. This is one of the best books on ethics. It is written in the same style of the *One Minute Manager* series and is a great addition to your business library.

a copy of this poem with me since I was in college as a reminder of what is important and have included it here for you. Thanks to Drs. Blanchard and Peale, I now know the author of the poem.

### The Man in The Glass by Dale Wimbrow

When you get what you want in our struggle for self
    And the world makes you king for a day
Just go to the mirror and look at yourself
    And see what that man has to say.

For it isn't your father or mother or wife
    Whose judgment upon you must pass,
The fellow whose verdict counts most in your life
    Is the man looking back in the glass.

Some people may think you a straight shooting chum
    And call you a wonderful guy,
But the man in the glass says you're only a bum
    If you can't look him straight in the eye.

He's the fellow to please, never mind all the rest,
    For he's with you clear up to the end
And you've passed your most dangerous, difficult test
    If the man in the glass is your friend.

You may fool the whole world down the pathway of life
    And get pats on the back as you pass,
But your only reward will be heartaches and tears
    If you've cheated the man in the glass.

Jerry Clower, the great country comedian, once told a crowd in Augusta, Georgia, "If you have to think about it, you are fixing to mess up." The same is true with ethics. If you have to wonder if it is ethical to do something—do not do it.

**Attitude**. The attitude of the leader sets the tone for the entire organization. A true leader has to have a positive outlook to lead the organization in the right direction and ensure that all change is an improvement. It only takes about two weeks for your attitude to pass from you to your employees to your customers. Dick Vermeil once stated that, "There is only one thing more contagious than a good attitude, that is a bad attitude." Your organization is better off if they catch a good attitude from you.

The other aspect of attitude is that in the supply chain business, or any business for that matter is that we must all remember that regardless of what business we think we are in, we are in the people business. General Patton tells us, "My theory is that an Army Commander does what is necessary to accomplish his mission, and that nearly eighty percent of his mission is to arouse morale in his men." The best way to raise the morale of the employee is to listen to them when they have ideas, problems or concerns.

Another excellent way to raise the morale of the employee is for them to see you. General U.S. Grant applied this technique repeatedly during the American Civil War. In the early 1990s, there was a plethora of articles and books about "Management by Wandering Around" (MBWA).[3] Management experts touted this technique as the latest management fad. However, this technique should have been called "Leadership by Wandering Around." It is by "wandering around" that the employees know who you are and know that you are concerned about them and their work conditions.

A good leader should be seen as often as possible in the work areas. To improve the morale of the employee and know what is going on, a good leader has to get out of the office and personally see and be seen. Gus Pagonis, the Chief Logistician at Sears, does this throughout the Sears logistics operations. One of his policies is that all of his leadership team has to spend a set number of days each year working on the floor, in the stock room, or in the distribution center. This allows the leaders to see what is going on and to fix the problems that they encounter. Southwest Airlines, one of the few profitable airlines today, has a similar policy for all of its employees. "Employees participate in a program called a 'a day in the field,' where they work in other positions to understand the jobs that

---

3.    The concept of "Management by Wondering Around" was developed at Hewlett-Packard. The business world became aware of this technique through the works of Tom Peters and Robert Waterman, primarily through *In Search of Excellence*.

their fellow employees do." [4] This is how you improve the Attitude of the workers. You cannot lead from behind the computer screen.

A critical virtue of a leader is to know himself/herself and to know the competition, as well as the employees. The only way to know the employees is to "wander around" and talk to them. The boost in employee morale and attitude is well worth the time. Too often managers will not leave the comfort of their offices to see what is happening and who is doing what. This is one of the attributes and qualities that separate a leader from a manager.

The attitude of the leadership team sets the tone for the entire organization. A leader that gets out of the office and personally observes what is going on in the distribution centers, warehouses, and shop floors will be in a better position to make decisions and will garner more Loyalty from the employees.

**Devotion**. A leader's devotion has to be to his/her employees and to the organization. Another critical devotion that managers and leaders often neglect is the devotion to their families. A recent country and western song contained the line, "I've never seen a headstone with these words: 'If only I had spent more time at work.'" Too many leaders preach the need to have a balance between work and family and then violate the principle themselves. Do not just preach the need for balance. Demonstrate to your employees that you are following your own guidance. They are watching closely how well you follow what you preach.

**Employees**. They are our responsibility to take care of, train, develop, and mentor. In the military, the requirement to take care of the "employees" is a little more critical than in the commercial world. Nevertheless, in both environments it is important to establish a work environment that is safe and free of prejudices.

Leaders have to understand what is going on in the lives of their employees to effectively lead them. Steven Covey, in his book *7 Habits of Highly Effective People*, says it best when he discusses the habit, "Seek first to understand and then be understood."

The leader must have empathy for his/her employees and their families—the leader must display a genuine concern for the employees and families. This genuine concern is what assists in developing the loyalty from the bottom up. Sun Tzu tells us, "If people are treated with benevolence, faithfulness, and justice, then they will be of one mind and will be glad to serve."

A leader's concern for the morale, health, and welfare of his/her employees cannot be faked. It has to be real and genuine. Today's employees are smart

---

4.    Wright, K.R., *The Few The Proud The Bankrupt*, Biddle Publishing Company, Brunswick, ME, 2000, p.145.

enough to know when the leaders are fictitious and do not really care about them. True concern for the employees also helps to develop the first quality of loyalty.

One of the most important qualities of a leader associated with empathy is listening. Listening to your employees is critical to learning not only what is important to them but also what areas may need your attention for supply chain improvements. Have you ever wondered why you have two ears and only one mouth? Perhaps this is because you should listen twice as much as you talk.

**Respect**. Respect for employees and co-workers are necessary for a productive work environment. Although a leader must earn respect, the respect for subordinates must be constantly present. There is a difference between the respect for a position and the respect for the person in that position. You have to strive to earn the personal respect afforded your job or position. It is more important to the success of your supply chain to earn respect from your subordinates for your abilities to produce results and take care of them than just to be respected for your position.

**Supportive**. Leadership support to subordinates comes in the form of personal and professional support. One of the successes of the Army is the genuine concern that leaders show for subordinates and their families. This ties back to the quality of empathy and attitude.

**Humor**. The ability to laugh is an important trait for leaders. This includes the ability to laugh at you. Every one makes mistakes every single day. Some of these quaffs are humorous. Your employees will think so; therefore if it is funny, laugh.

**Integrity**. This is not negotiable for leaders to be successful. Once a leader compromises his/her integrity, they also compromise their ability to lead effectively. This has to be the essential attribute when looking for new leaders and employees. In the article, "Becoming a Star in Your Organization,"[5] posted to the Sonshi.com website, the author states, "There is nothing that will destroy your worth as a person more than dishonesty…When you encounter a situation where you have to decide on whether to take a path of the straight and narrow versus the crooked and wide, just remember that someone is bound to find out about your choice eventually. And if you have children, what decision would you want your kids to make if they were in your shoes?" If your employees do not have faith in you to be honest and straightforward with them, you will not be success-

---

5.   Sonshi.com, http://www.sonshi.com/star.html. Sonshi.com is a website devoted to the teachings of Sun Tzu. This website gives the owner's interpretation of the writings of Sun Tzu, interviews with leading authors, and articles on subjects related to the writings of Sun Tzu.

ful as a leader. In addition, if you have their trust, the quickest way to ruin an organization is to take an action that will cause them to lose this trust.

In recent times, the Enron scandal is an example of a lack integrity coupled with a greedy management team. A coach of a major college football program took actions that gave the appearance of a lapse in integrity and it cost him his job. Another major college coach, in a moment of questionable integrity, flowered up his resume and then with the facts brought to light, he, too, lost his new job. When the employees cannot trust a leader, whether real or perceived, the company will not be able to move forward to the next level of excellence. Integrity lapses have a tendency to grow like a cancer in an organization. The only way to get rid of the cancer is to cut it out and remove it from the organization. Make sure if you are getting rid of an employee to remove the cancerous growth that you replace the ousted leader with one with unquestionable integrity.

**Professional Pride**. This is an essential ingredient for a leader and an important attribute for leaders to instill in their subordinates. Leaders have to be willing to have their name "signed" to their work.

# What is leadership?

Is leadership a learned trait? Is leadership something that you can learn in the classroom? On the other hand, is it something that you have to learn "in the field?" Leaders are not born, they have to be taught and trained. Business management schools do a great job of training managers, however, many of them do not teach leadership. The schools that teach leadership provide the foundation but corporations need to accept the responsibility for the training of leaders to complement the teaching from the schools.

> *"Leadership is the thing that wins battles. I have it but I'll be damned if I can define it. It probably consists of what you want to do, and then doing it, and getting mad as hell if someone tries to get in your way. Self confidence and leadership are twin brothers."*
>
> —*George S. Patton, Jr.*[6]

Leadership is one of those overused, undefined words. Almost everyone believes they know what leadership is and can recognize it when they see it. However, they are not able to give leadership a definition. The Army defines it as:

---

6.    Ridge, Warren J., *Follow Me*, 1989, AMACOM, NY, p. 35.

"Leadership is **influencing** people—by providing purpose, direction, and motivation—while **operating** to accomplish the mission and improving the organization."[7]

Over time, the terms of leadership and management have become almost interchangeable because of the inability to define leadership as alluded to by General Patton. In the next part of this chapter, we will look at the difference between leaders and managers. During this discussion, we will look at why both are necessary and how leadership can improve Supply Chains and Supply Chain Management.

## *Leadership and Supply Chains*

To illustrate the need for these leadership qualities in supply chain operations let's look at an example from Operation Iraqi Freedom. All of the Meals, Ready to Eat (better known as MREs), prepackaged meals, and water support for the operations in Kuwait were supported from a single distribution center located at one of the Kuwaiti Ports. After several days of botched deliveries of rations and water, I visited the port facility to walk the process and see what the problem was. This visit was predicated on being a firm believer in the words of General Patton, when he said, "no effective decision was ever made from the seat of a swivel chair." What I discovered was a three-warehouse distribution center with no work going on. I was originally told that this was because there were no operational forklifts. At that time, as if by divine intervention, a forklift drove by, then another, and then I saw two more just sitting in the largest of the three warehouses. Both of which I soon discovered worked. The next excuse for not loading the containers was that only one soldier knew how to work a forklift and it would take him an hour to load a truck by himself. I then discovered the process to "load" one container. The process started by driving a military truck into the warehouse and a twenty-foot container was loaded onto the truck. A driver moved the truck outside the warehouse where a soldier using container-handling equipment removed the container from the military truck. The soldier then placed the container on the appropriate outgoing truck. The obvious question was, "Why not load the outgoing truck inside the warehouse and only move the container once?" To demonstrate, I got on the other forklift in the warehouse and started assisting in moving and loading the containers. After a few trucks, we had the process clicking. Just like any warehouse worker, these soldiers needed some

---

7.    US Army Field Manual 22-100, *Leadership*, 1999.

leadership, mentoring, training, and someone to show that they were concerned about getting the job done. By the next day when we visited again, every soldier at the port was working. The loading that took "an hour per truck" the day before now took eleven minutes per truck and there were three trucks being loaded at the same time.

## What are the responsibilities of a Supply Chain Leader?

A leader has the responsibility to provide a clearly understood mission statement and vision for the organization. The vision should establish the goals for the organization. The leader then must provide the necessary support. This includes facilities, assets, the right people, and financial support; setting the direction and the example; and then getting out of the way to let the people do the job.

A leader has to be able to get the best out of his/her employees. To do this, the leader has to possess the qualities listed earlier in this chapter and remember to focus on doing the right things, not just doing things right. You can do something right but if it is not the right course of action you have accomplished nothing.

## What is the difference between a leader and a manager?

The first real difference is that a manager focuses on doing things right and the leader focuses on doing the right things. A manager is concerned with managing resources and the leader is concerned with the people.

In his book, *The Few, The Proud, The Bankrupt,* [8] Dr. Kim Wright, who I had the honor of serving with in Kuwait, wrote a great example of a manager focusing on the short term bottom line and not the people:

"Martin Manager is one of the modern "B" school graduates with the bottom-line view of management. In his infinite wisdom he determines that one employee, Mike Mechanic, making $60,000 per year in salary with the correspondingly high cost of fringe benefits, is too expensive. Remember the airline mantra—reduce costs. Martin's solution to the cost reduction process approaches

---

8.    Wright, K.R., *The Few The Proud The Bankrupt*, Biddle Publishing Company, Brunswick, ME, 2000, p.20.

genius. By forcing Mike to quit or retire early, Martin can go out and buy three times the value by hiring three new mechanics with Mike's old salary. For a $20,000 per year salary with correspondingly low fringe benefits, Martin gets three mechanics for the price of one. What a genius, what a star, what a great future! Martin may be a success by traditional management standards but in reality, he cannot connect the dots. He cannot see beyond the now. He cannot fathom the intangibles, the *indirect costs* of his decision. Intangibles do not show up on the balance sheet. Or do they? Every mechanic on the ramp can tell you what these intangible costs are. For example, when Ned Newbee, one of Martin's new hire mechanics, tries to fix a problem on a 727 filled with revenue passengers at the gate five minutes prior to departure, we get the payoff. Due to cutbacks at the airline (more of the management's cost reductions), Ned is all by himself; and being relatively unfamiliar with his work, he is proceeding by following the maintenance manual instructions. All goes well until Ned makes one small mistake that destroys a critical part, which will cost the airline over $100,000 to replace. Now, not only is the original part not fixed, but now the airplane isn't going anywhere for some time to come. The result is the aircraft is removed from service, passengers are deplaned, and either put on a competitor's planes or sent to hotels. Both options come at a substantial cost.

This mistake could cost the airline up to $150,000-$200,000 and will never be traced to the decision by Martin Manager."

How many managers trained to cut costs would make the same decision. You would be surprised at the number of times this happens in industry. In the 1980's and 1990's, one prominent Florida firm made this type of decision on a regular basis to keep "costs" down. Every four to five years they would have a layoff and then a few months later hire replacements at a much-discounted salary to do the same job. What is lost in this discussion is the focus on the people. This is the difference between the leader and the manager.

At this point folks usually ask, "Wouldn't the leader make a decision on cost savings?" The answer is yes; the leader would indeed make a decision on cost savings that could very well result in layoffs of trained personnel. But, first the leader would analyze the impacts on the company and the employees involved and would not make the less than ethical decision of replacing one trained employee with three untrained. Lost in the "cost" equation in the above reference is the cost to train the new employee to the same level of experience of the old employee forced to leave early.

In the movie *G.I. Jane,* the Senior Master Chief told the trainees, "There are no bad crews, only bad leaders." Is there such a thing as a bad leader? Alternatively, is it just a manager trying to do a leader's job? I would suggest that it could be a combination of both. Corporate America has spent a fortune over the past several decades to find and recruit the right employees from the major business schools. However, most business curriculums do not contain leadership courses. Moreover, all too often, we make the mistake of assuming that an educated manager can be a leader with no additional training.

How does a leader take his/her organization to a new level of excellence? I do not profess to have all of the answers in this area. I can only tell you what works for me and has proven to work in both wartime and peacetime assignments.

- **Get out of the Office!** Remember the words of General Patton. You have to get out of the swivel chair and walk the process to know what is really happening in the supply chain or the shop floor.

- **Talk to the workers and LISTEN.** The essential action here is to listen when the employees talk.

- **Spend time doing the work to understand the conditions.** All too often, as we climb the corporate ladder, we forget what is important to the workers. In Kuwait, I was able to get on the forklifts and do the work in the Theater Distribution Center. I realize that OSHA regulations would probably frown on that in the United States. However, spending a day or two on a regular basis doing the actual work will give you a whole new perspective on what your workers are doing and the conditions that they are doing it in. This is a new twist to Covey's seek first concept. Seek to understand the work and the conditions.

- **Understand your supply chain's processes.** The only way to know and understand the processes is to get out of the office and physically walk the process and ask questions on what is going on and why.

- **Ask questions: the five whys.** Usually by asking why five times you will get to the root cause of a problem or find out why a process is done the way that it is.

- **Solve problems.** Once you understand the processes and listen to the employees, take action to make it better.

- **Walk the process often!** Are you starting to get the idea that this is important?

How does this tie to Supply Chain Excellence? The leader has to understand the process, provide a vision of the destination situation, benchmark the improvements, use After Action Reviews to seek improvement without placing the blame on an individual or section, and has to know the business. Leadership is what takes an average supply chain and makes it a great supply chain. Without it, process improvements in supply chains are not possible.

# 3

# *Supply Chain Lessons from the Ancient Writings of Sun-Tzu*

Who is Sun Tzu and how does he relate to Supply Chain Management? Depending on the translation, Sun Tzu either was a great warrior, a compilation of several writers in Ancient China or did not exist at all. Again, depending on the translator, Sun Tzu lived between the 500s BC and the mid-200s BC. The consensus opinion is that he did indeed exist and lived in the Wu Dynasty and came to prominence around 519 BC and slipped into obscurity before his death.

Throughout the writings of Sun-Tzu are the threads of Leadership, Communications, Planning and Preparation, and Discipline. This chapter will look at these threads in light of the following areas: Matters of vital importance, Clearly stated missions, know yourself, speed, competition, the importance of remaining current, the use of after action reviews (AARs), and collaboration as they apply to supply chain management and supply chain leadership.

The writings of Sun Tzu were first translated into the western world by French missionaries between 1772 and the early 1790's. This is significant in that it is known that Napoleon Bonaparte studied these translation and its applications can be seen in the battles of Jena and Austerlitz. During the Napoleonic Wars, Baron Henri Jomini and Karl Von Clausewitz served as both allies and opponents of Napoleon at various times. During Napoleon's time, as during the times of Sun Tzu, loyalty was fleeting and could be bought. The ability to buy a leader's loyalty is how Jomini and Clausewitz served as allies and opponents of Napoleon. Jomini and Clausewitz wrote on the tactics and strategy of Napoleon. These writings formed the basis for today's modern military thought and in fact, the modern principles of war came from these writings.

The Secretary of Defense, Donald Rumsfeld, and the Commander of the United States Central Command, General Tommy Franks, both quoted Sun Tzu during the course of Operation Iraqi Freedom. Sun Tzu has become a staple in the United States Military Officer Education System and is studied in the Command and Staff Colleges (Intermediate Officer Education System) and in the Senior Service Colleges (Advanced Military Education). The Command and Staff College is a military requirement for promotion to Lieutenant Colonel/Commander and the Senior Service College is a requirement for promotion to Flag Officer (General/Admiral).

The writings of Sun Tzu are more than 2500 years old and yet they are as applicable today as they were when they were written. Sun Tzu wrote *The Art of War* in a universal style that lends itself to templates. This is why bookstores carry numerous versions of *The Art of War* translated to topics from financial management to business management. Using the universal and template style we will look at the writings of Sun Tzu and their applicability to Supply Chain Management.

Examples of Sun Tzu can be seen in the writings of Mao Tse Tung, the strategy of Ho Chi Minh and the Viet Cong. The Japanese attack at Pearl Harbor (the use of spies, deception, and attacking where unexpected) is an example of applying the teachings of Sun Tzu. The Nazi High Command also studied and applied the writings during World War II (attacking when unexpected at the Battle of the Bulge and attacking the will to fight by bombing London). The Japanese business books of the 20th Century reflect the influence of his writings.

Good examples of Sun Tzu in practice in US military operations include Operation Desert Storm and Operation Iraqi Freedom. During Desert Storm, the US Marines continued to practice beach landings under the watchful eye of CNN. This gave the Iraqi leadership the distinct impression that the attack to free Kuwait would indeed come from the sea. During this time, the US Seventh Corps moved through the desert to conduct an end around run to pin the Iraqi forces down and then defeat them.

During Iraqi Freedom, the use of speed and deception produced a much shorter war with much fewer casualties than expected. This application of Sun Tzu's teachings also allowed the coalition forces to capture the Rumallah oil fields before an environmental disaster could be started in the form of burning oil wells.

## Sun Tzu and Supply Chains

In the second chapter of *The Art of War*, Sun Tzu states, "War is a matter of vital importance to the state; the province of life of death; the road to survival or ruin. It is mandatory that it be thoroughly studied." Few would argue that Supply Chain Management is a matter of vital importance to any company. It is indeed the road to survival or ruin. The biggest cause of failure for the dot.coms was a failure to establish a clear supply chain strategy. One major toy chain paid more in coupons to compensate for late deliveries at Christmas a couple of years ago than they made in profit. Truly, leaders of all companies to ensure that the most efficient supply chain operations are in place and to posture the company for survival and growth and not ruin must study supply chain management.

What are matters of supply chain management? The matters of importance to supply chains and to corporations are those items that are of vital importance to the customers. It is imperative for survival of the company that these items are benchmarked internally and against the competition to ensure that you can provide the good or service better and faster than the customer desires and better than the competition. If what you are measuring is not important to the customer and to customer support, it should not be important to the company. If it is not important to the company do not measure it.

> *"The Grand Duke said…. One who is confused in purpose cannot respond to his enemy (III.23)."*

Sun Tzu is talking about the importance of clearly stated missions. The words of the Grand Duke can easily be translated into—to know your purpose, you must have a clearly stated mission and vision. This vision and mission has to be clearly stated, clearly articulated, and most important of all, clearly understood at all levels of the organization. Sun Tzu said, "Knowledge that does not go beyond what the generals know is not good." If not all levels of the organization understand the mission, it is of no value to the organization. One of Sun Tzu's rules for finding a good leader was "see who is able to make rules clear and commands easy to follow." President Ronald Reagan is a good example of a leader that was able to make commands easy to follow. Another good example of a clearly articulated mission was the guidance from President George H.W. Bush for Operation Desert Storm. His mission was clearly articulated and understood throughout the world as simply "to get the Iraqis out of Kuwait".

Leadership is responsible for ensuring that the mission is clear and provides the vision necessary to get the organization moving forward. A large specialty retailer discovered that the lack of clarity in the need to have a fully understood mission for supply chain visibility resulted in an extra $38 million in daily inventory in their supply chain. A fully understood mission on supply chain visibility corrected this.

The supply chain leadership is also responsible for establishing and articulating fully understood goals throughout the company. If you are setting goals that do not consider the impacts of each link of the supply chain, you create confusion within the company. Goals that are not clearly articulated and fully understood may lead to less than optimal performance for the company. Vague goals may in fact appear to encourage local optimizations counter to the goals of the overall supply chain.

One drug firm learned this lesson the hard way. Their supply chain goals rewarded traffic managers for maximizing full truckload deliveries from their distribution centers. When they did a full accounting of the supply chain goals and missions, they discovered that one traffic manager was rewarded for saving $25 per truckload by waiting until the trucks were full truckloads. The result was an additional $500K in interest charges.

The Army learned the same thing when they changed the accounting and billing practices for tank engines. In the mid 1990s, the Army established a financial policy that rewarded individual installations for "entrepreneurship" in managing major repair parts such as engines. This program made it more attractive to rebuild engines rather than buy a new one. In the short run, this looked good to the installations—a choice between replacing one of the four modules of the engine for $125K and buying a new engine for $500K. In the short run, installations were able to save a few dollars but the practice of replacing the modules skewed the demand data and forecasting models for tank engines. In addition, this practice resulted in soldiers having to replace multiple modules over the course of time. Every time the engine had problems, it had to be pulled out. The mechanic then removed the bad module and replaced it with a new one. This very time consuming process takes almost as long as replacing the engine itself. It is analogous to putting a new patch on an old pair of jeans, the first time you wash the jeans the hole is bigger. When you put a new module on an old core, soon the other three modules are not as strong and you will end up replacing them as well. The Army recently changed the financial accounting policies to rectify this suboptimizing policy.

## Supply Chain Leadership

Supply chain leadership is distinctly different from supply chain management. A tour through any local bookstore will reveal an average of six times more shelf space for books on management than leadership. To date the subject of supply chain leadership has not been a hot topic. Leadership is necessary to move a company to a new level of excellence. Leadership is about people not assets. Keynote presentations at major logistics conferences always address a company's management team; annual reports address the management teams' positions and goals. What is missing is leadership. Sun Tzu did not miss talking about leadership. Leadership is one of the threads woven throughout the writings of Sun Tzu. Sun Tzu preached and wrote about character-based leadership.

In the first chapter Sun Tzu said, "If people are treated with benevolence, faithfulness, and justice, then they will be of one mind and will be glad to serve." All a worker wants out of a job is fair treatment and to have the faith of his/her co-workers and supervisors.

In Chapter 8, Sun Tzu gives guidance on leadership traits. He said, "Good Generals act in accord with events—not quick to anger, not subjected to embarrassment. When they see possibility, they are like tigers. Their action and inaction are matters of strategy." Good supply chain leaders are the same—they are slow to anger. The true leader does not need to raise his voice, shout, and scream. The Army does not have a monopoly on this style of leadership. Too many officers believe that the best way to get a point across is to yell at subordinates and loose their temper. Leaders have to set the example so that they are above embarrassment and above embarrassing their employees in public. Because the leaders have planned ahead, they are ready to take action when an opportunity appears.

In Chapter 3, Sun Tzu tells us, "Generals are the assistants of the nation. When their assistance is complete (defined as good and wise; loyal and capable), the country is strong. When their assistance is defective, the country is weak....Those whose upper and lower ranks have the same desire are victorious." Supply chain leaders are truly the assistants of the corporation. When the supply chain leaders are strong, wise, and loyal, the company is strong. When the leaders are weak or exhibit lack of loyalty the company is weak. Strong leaders enable a victorious company by developing and fostering a corporate culture.

The US Marine Corps are the world-class benchmark for developing a corporate culture. There are no "ex-marines." The US Marine Corps indoctrinates every single recruit in the history and customs of the Marine Corps before any other training is completed. After a complete immersion in the history and customs, the recruits learn how to be a Marine. Upon completion of basic training, the recruit receives his/her insignia for his/her uniform.[1] This rite of passage to

---

1.    The Army started a similar rite of passage for recruits when they graduate from their training programs. Upon graduation, the recruits are awarded their coveted black beret.

become a Marine leaves each Marine with the indoctrination of "once a Marine, always a Marine." Ask a Soldier what he/she is and they will tell you that he/she is a mechanic, an infantryman, or a tanker. Ask a Marine and he/she will tell you "I am a Marine!"

A corporate culture is important to the supply chain to ensure that everyone has a shared set of values. Just as every Marine shares the same "corporate" culture, each of the workers in your company should have a shared corporate culture. How much training do your employees get on the history and culture of your company?

In Chapter 6 the words of Sun Tzu tell us, "The power of those united is whole, while the power of those who are divided is reduced." Corporate culture and shared values assist in uniting the whole. Since *The Art of War* was not translated into English until the early 20<sup>th</sup> Century, it is safe to assume that Abe Lincoln never read Sun Tzu. However, these words sound remarkably like the words of Lincoln, "A house divided against itself cannot stand." Early in his book (in Chapter 1), Sun Tzu tells us, if leaders can be "humane and just, sharing both the gains and the troubles of the people, then the troops will be loyal and naturally identify with the interests" of the leadership. It is documented that General Patton did read Sun Tzu as part of his personal professional development. Moreover, if George were here today he would probably tell you that not only did he read Sun Tzu but that he served with him, too. General Patton said, "No effective decision was ever made from the seat of a swivel chair." What Patton and Sun Tzu are telling us is that leaders have to get out of the office, leave the computer screen and see what is really happening on the shop or warehouse floor. During Operation Iraqi Freedom, I frequently got on a forklift to pull orders, move pallets, and load trucks to see what the weather conditions were doing to productivity at the Theater Distribution Center. By doing this, I was able to understand the great reduction in productivity created by the 50 mile per hour sandstorms. I was able to see first hand that these conditions required an additional guide on the truck being loaded and a ground guide for the forklift operators to ensure that safety was maintained.

Sun Tzu tells us that disorder will result from a General that is "morally weak" and without discipline. During the previous administration, the Army was not in disorder but the actions of a Commander in Chief who was morally weak did indeed create a loss of morale throughout the military. The leadership of Enron and Arthur Andersen Accounting are other examples of the results of morally weak leadership. The ripple affects of the leadership of these two companies are classic examples of the impact of morally weak leaders. Their actions affected not only on the company but also on the employees of the company and the companies with whom they did business.

Leaders have to set the example. They have to provide vision that is understood. They must provide supply chain leadership, discipline, and training. In all operations it is true that Standards lead to habits, habits lead to discipline, and with discipline, all things are possible. The supply chain leaders must set the standards and then follow them.

"The supreme importance in war is to attack the enemy's strategy." The supreme importance in supply chain management is to have a supply chain strategy that will meet the needs of the customer. Do you have a supply chain strategy? What is it? Do your employees understand it? What are your strategic objectives? What is the strategic advantage of your supply chain? Is it quality, responsiveness, and/or customer support? If you are not focusing on what is important to the customer, you are focusing on the wrong things and it is time to reevaluate your supply chain strategy.

Therefore, leaders who understand strategy "preside over the destiny of the people and determine the stability or instability" of their organization. In order to lead your company to new levels of excellence, you have to understand the supply chain strategy of your organization. In addition, you must be able to articulate this strategy to your employees in such a way that they fully understand it also.

Sun Tzu tells us that the strength or weakness of a company depends on the quality of its leaders. Because of this, it is important to take great care in selecting people for positions of responsibility. This is as true today as it was 2500 years ago when Sun Tzu wrote it. Just because a person is a good manager does not ensure that that person will be a good leader. Being the boss' favorite does not ensure a quality leader.

## *Know Yourself*

"Know your enemy, know yourself; in a hundred battles you will never be in peril." Sun Tzu tells us to be invincible you must know yourself and must assess yourself and your competition in the following 5 areas:

1.   **The Way**—this is the vision that we spoke of earlier.

2.   **The Weather**—in military operations the weather is an uncontrollable variable that can be an advantage or disadvantage. In business, there are uncontrollable variables as well. If your plan and vision incorporates contingency

planning, you will be prepared to take advantage of the uncontrollable variables. These factors include: the economy, the growth phases of a company or product, and the acceptance of a new product.

3.  **The Terrain**—in military operations the terrain like the weather can be an advantage or a disadvantage. You have to consider the business terrain of your supply chain operations. In the military, there is "no-go/slow-go" terrain such as swamps and high mountains. In business, there are also areas of operations that are "no-go/slow-go" terrains that one should avoid. Proper planning and knowing yourself will enable you to avoid such terrain and/or use the terrain to your advantage.

4.  **The leadership**—we have covered leadership in depth from the perspective of Sun Tzu, another chapter will cover leadership in more detail.

5.  **The discipline**—remember with discipline all things are possible.

What is the best way to know yourself? My experience tells me the best way to see and know yourself is through the use of detailed process maps or flow charts. The only way to develop an accurate flow chart of your processes is to get out of the "swivel chair" and physically walk the process. Take the action from the beginning until the end. In the Army, we charted the actions necessary to go from a soldier ordering a part or item of supply through the supply chain until the part or item of supply was received and used by the soldier. While walking the process it is important to ask why—the rule of thumb is by the fifth why you will discover the root cause of the problem. While asking why it is important to document the actions and results of every process in the chain and the time necessary to accomplish the actions. In addition, look for actions that are non-value added. If there were no value to the action, why would you want to do it? Knowing yourself is important for your individual processes such as job changes, promotions, and retirements.

# *Speed*

"Speed is the essence of warfare." Unarguably, speed is the essence of supply chain management. Speed in supply chains can take the form of faster cycle times, faster customer order times, faster customer response times, faster to the market, or even faster out of a non-profitable market. The key here is not to confuse speed with doing something hastily. There is a big difference. It should allow you to reduce the piles of supplies because of the information and speed of your supply chain. Remember that sometimes faster is not necessarily faster. During Operation Iraqi Freedom, the Patriot Air Defense folks decided that they could get parts faster by calling back to their "sources" in the United States rather than depend on the established distribution system. They arranged for shipment of their parts on the next available premium delivery service coming from the United States to Kuwait. This option would have their parts in country "five hours earlier" than could the formal distribution system. Their plane did indeed leave five hours earlier than the scheduled plane. What they did not do was to look at the information on the delivery routes. Their plane went through Bahrain and their parts remained in Bahraini Customs for two days and then spent time in the Kuwaiti Customs. The part they needed was also shipped via the established distribution system and arrived three days earlier than the "faster" shipment.

# *Competition*

Sun Tzu's guidance on competition tells us, "If your troops do not equal his, temporarily avoid his initial on rush." If you are taking on a competitor head to head, make sure you are ready for his/her initial on rush. To do this you have to be prepared (another of the threads woven throughout *The Art of War*). Let us look at some examples of not being prepared to take on the competition. Many of the dot.com companies were obviously not prepared to take on the established brick and mortar companies in the supply chain arena resulting in their demise. Home Depot and Lowe's is another example. Growing up in North Carolina the only home improvement store was Lowe's. Then along comes The Home Depot with more than 1000 stores in 20 years and the fastest company to hit $150 billion in sales. Lowe's had to assess its strategy, which appeared for several years to be open a new store within a few blocks of a Home Depot, and take them on head to head. When Lowe's reassessed their strategy, they realized that females start the majority of home improvement projects. This prompted Lowe's to start carrying more pastels, more furniture, and more appliances in their stores. This allowed them to increase their stock price by 82% over a two-year period. The Home Depot counter to this was to go into the appliance business. After less than two years, Home Depot is now the third largest retailer of appliances.

K-Mart and Wal-Mart are another example of not being prepared to take on a competitor head to head. Again, back to my experience growing up in North Carolina, there were the top end stores—Ivey's (now Dillard's), Talheimers' (now Hecht's), the middle tier stores such as Penney's and Sears, and the only one discount retailer—K-Mart. The way I play golf, there was no need to go to the more expensive stores for my clubs, shoes, and golf balls. After all, with the number that I lost every round why buy the expensive balls. Therefore, I shopped at K-Mart in Raleigh for my golfing needs.[2] Along comes Wal-Mart and becomes the largest retailer in the world and K-Mart is stuck searching for a strategy to compete. They tried matching supply chains but could not compete with Wal-Mart. Then K-Mart seized on the idea of a "whatever you buy we will take it back no questions asked" returns policy to compete. This resulted in $980 million in returns the last year before K-Mart declared bankruptcy. They discovered that customers were buying items such as lawn mowers, using them for the season and then bringing them back in the fall for a full refund. Their inability to compete and the lack of preparation to do so resulted in one of the largest bankruptcy filings in US history.

## *Training and Remaining Current*

"If officers are unaccustomed to rigorous training they will be worried and hesitant in battle." The only way to ensure that your leaders are not hesitant in the face of competition or decisions is to ensure that they receive the proper training. In the Army, we have the National Training Center at Fort Irwin, California, with the sole mission of training leaders in realistic desert combat against a well-trained opponent and live fire training against computer-controlled targets. The US Marines do the same type of training at Twenty-Nine Palms in Southern California. The successes of Operation Desert Storm and Operation Iraqi Freedom validated the quality of the training at these two training centers. Sun Tzu tells us to look past "rustics" and that the greatest of crimes is not to prepare while the greatest virtues is to be prepared for any contingency. The purpose of these two training centers is to prepare soldiers for any contingency on the battlefield.

Just as the military invests millions of dollars annually to prepare soldiers for any contingency in combat operations, companies have to be willing to invest in training for their employees to ensure success in business operations. Toyota

---

2.    An interesting note on K-Mart and Wal-Mart is that both of them were founded in 1962. However, it was not until the late 1970s that K-Mart starting moving into the smaller markets controlled by Wal-Mart. In his autobiography, Sam Walton admits that a majority of his ideas for Wal-Mart operations came from visiting K-Marts and copying and improving on what he saw.

invested $50 Million in the University of Toyota to ensure employees receive the proper training necessary for success.

There is a difference between training and education. Education is a classroom type of learning and is important. However, training is a hands on form of learning. Toyota requires every employee at its Ontario, CA parts distribution center to have eighty hours of training every year. Two full weeks of training every year for every employee. This is one of the reasons that the retention rate is exceeds 95% since the distribution center was opened in 1996. The Army requires every leader to attend refresher training at preplanned intervals throughout their career to ensure that the leaders remain current and relevant.

Another essential area of training is cross training. This form of training is critical for supply chain success. Nothing is more frustrating to a customer than to ask for assistance or ask a question only to be told that the person that does that is on vacation and no one else is trained to do that action.

## *The Use of After Action Reviews*

"Therefore, when I have won a victory I do not repeat my tactics but respond to circumstances in an infinite variety of ways." What Sun Tzu is telling us here is to change our tactics and look at what we did right and what we did wrong. In the Army, we use a process known as the After Action Review. We use this process after every training event and every operation to determine what went right according to the plan and what went wrong and why. This process design is not to fix blame for something going wrong but to find out WHY something went wrong and how to prevent it from happening again. The After Action Review process can be a lengthy process, a very detailed process, or a hasty process. An After Action Review could be as simple as Gus Pagonis' 3x5 card version with three ups and three downs. The importance of this version is being able to answer the question—"how do we sustain the ups? And how do we fix and prevent the downs?"

The Army's After Action Review process is a straightforward approach to getting to the root cause of the problem. It is a seven-step process:

1.  What was the plan?

2.  What actually happened? Did we follow the plan?

3.  What went right? How do we sustain that?

4.   What went wrong?

5.   Why?

6.   How do we fix it?

7.   Who is responsible for ensuring that it is fixed?

The keys to the success of the After Action Review process are honesty and the final two steps. You will notice that **Who** messed up is not a point here. The focus is what went wrong and how do we fix it. The final step is assigning a person or office the responsibility for ensuring that the problem is fixed. Remember the old adage: we only do well what the boss is checking. Without responsibility, the problem there is a good chance the same problem will surface again and we will respond in the same manner again. In combat operations, repeating the same mistakes could mean the loss of lives. In business, repeating the same mistakes could mean the loss of customers and eventually the loss of the company itself.

## *Collaboration/Mergers*

"Replace the enemy's flags and banners with your own, mix the captured chariots with yours—treat the captives well and care for them." If you merge with another company or buy them out, ensure that the employees of the company are all treated the same. If you have a company uniform make sure that on day one everyone is in the uniform of the parent company. Failure to do so results in confusion for the customer and morale problems for the employees. One example of not having the new employees in the right uniform happened at Fort Irwin when a new contract started. The contractor went for the lowest bidder and for the first two weeks of operations, the new employees were in a mix of old uniforms, new uniforms, and no uniforms. The assimilation of "captured" employees into the old company was one of the reasons the Roman Empire flourished and survived for so long. They assimilated captured soldiers into the Roman Army and in some instances made them Roman citizens.

## *Conclusions and Applications of Sun Tzu Today*

Sun Tzu gives us a common sense approach to leadership and supply chains. His words are as true today as they were 2500 years ago when they were first written. Sun Tzu tells us that we must know ourselves. Getting out of the office and seeing what is really happening in our supply chains is the best way to accomplish this. You must develop a detailed process map of your processes. This will give you a good tool for training your employees as well as improving your supply chain and customer service. Know yourself and know your processes and you will be successful in supply chain leadership.

Throughout *The Art of War*, Sun Tzu provides us with the qualities of leaders and gives us examples of how leaders should act. He reminds us that supply chain leaders are truly the keys to success or ruin of a corporation.

When the successful supply chain leader discovers a problem or a plan does not proceed as expected, Sun Tzu tells us to conduct an After Action Review to determine why the plan did not work.

What Sun Tzu shows us through his ancient writings is that as far as we have come in the past 2500 years with advances in technologies and customer demands for faster service, the basics of leadership and root cause analysis for problems will still lead you to the top.

# 4

# *Applying the Military Decision Making Process to Solving Supply Chain Problems*

The military uses a set methodology for planning operations. This methodology formed the framework for planning for Desert Storm and more recently for Operation Enduring Freedom and Operation Iraqi Freedom. This chapter looks at uses for this methodology in solving supply chain problems.

There are many methods of solving problems and developing plans for improvements. One such method is the Military Decision Making Process. This process is a multi-step process that provides leaders at all levels the ability to carefully analyze the situation and come to a logical decision on a course of action or an alternative. Even within the military, there is confusion on the Decision Making Process Model. This model does not make the decision for you; it is a tool to guide the user to making the logical decision. In supply chains, the wrong decision can be the difference in profits or losses; in the military, the wrong decision can be the difference between life and death. In business, too many wrong decisions can lead to the death of the company.

This chapter provides the background of the Military Decision Making Process and the steps involved in leading to a logical decision. Not only will this chapter show you some applications of this model to supply chain situations but also an example of how the model can be applied to personal situations, as well.

There is a number of problem solving methods available to today's supply chain practitioner. Corporate employees use some of these on a daily basis in the performance of their jobs. Among the most popular techniques are the Theory of

Constraints and Six Sigma[1] methodologies (for more on six sigma, please see Chapter 5). Another very popular problem solving method in some organizations is to do nothing and hope the problem will go away. Most of the companies that adopt the do nothing methodology end up doing nothing because their company goes out of business.

The Military Decision Making Process model is an analytical model that assists the user in knowing if a decision is necessary. The model will then guide the user as to when and what the decision should be. The model uses a logical sequence of steps to guide the user through this process.

Before delving into the model itself, it is prudent to define decision-making. US Army Field Manual 101-5, *Staff Operations*, states, "decisions are the means by which the commander translates his vision of the end state into action."[2] The American Heritage Dictionary defines a decision as: "The act of reaching a conclusion or making up one's mind."[3] The Military Decision Making Process will not make up one's mind. It will assist in reaching a logical decision. The key to the success of applying the Military Decision Making Process model is that it develops the leader in how to think and not what to think.

The Military Decision Making Process helps leaders to examine a situation and reach logical decisions. It assists the leader by allowing the leader to apply thoroughness, clarity, sound judgment, logic, and professional knowledge to reach a decision. The model is a detailed, deliberate, and sequential process when time allows. When time is critical as it sometimes is in war, as well as in making supply chain decisions, an abbreviated version of the model can be used. Some of the advantages of this model over other methodologies for problem solving are:

- It analyzes and compares multiple courses of action to identify the best possible action.

- It produces integration, coordination, and synchronization for an operation.

- The model minimizes overlooking critical aspects by looking at multiple actions and reactions.

---

1.   Six sigma is a methodology first used by Motorola to improve their quality. The literal application of Six Sigma is striving towards no more than 3.2 errors per one million transactions or items produced.
2.   US Army Field Manual 101-5, *Staff Operations*.
3.   *American Heritage College Dictionary*, Houghton Mifflin Company, Boston, 1997, p. 359.

- When followed the Military Decision Making Process model results in detailed plan.

- This model provides a common framework that enables parallel planning at multiple echelons.

*The military decision making process is a means to an end—the real value lies in the result and not the process.*[4]

The steps of the Military Decision Making Process as applied to Supply Chain problem solving are:

- Receipt of the Mission

- Mission Analysis

- Course of Action Development

- Course of Action Analysis

- Course of Action Comparison

- Course of Action Approval

- Orders production

The first step in the process is the receipt of the mission or identification of the problem. This requires determining exactly what is expected or what is not going as planned if identifying a problem. This can be passed down from corporate or from another source of information. Once the mission has been received or the problem identified an initial assessment of the situation is necessary to determine the guidance that will be passed to subordinates for action and analysis. In the military, the result of the initial assessment results in the commander's initial guidance. This may include additional tasks to be completed in order to complete the mission or additional areas to look at to determine the true nature of the problem.

The second step in the process is the mission analysis. This is where the staff kicks in high gear. What does the boss really need to know? What is the intent of the higher headquarters and what do they really expect of us in this situation? How does this problem or mission influence my area of responsibility? Each area

---

4.    US Army Field Manual 3-0, *Operations*, 2001.

of the staff should be working both independently on their area of expertise and jointly with the other staff areas to ensure that any impacts in one area is fully understood by the other staff members. The steps in the mission analysis phase are:

1.  Analyze the Higher Headquarters' order or the problem identified.

2.  Determine the specified, implied, and essential tasks. What was specifically in the higher headquarters' order for us to do? What is implied that needs to be done in order to meet the mission requirements or solve the problem that has been identified? Which tasks are essential to completion of the mission or solving the problem?

3.  Review of available assets to accomplish the mission or solve the problem. Here is where the "troop to task" analysis is important. Are there sufficient workers? Is there enough equipment and supplies?

4.  What are the constraints that limit the ability to successfully solve the problem or complete the mission?

5.  What are the critical facts and assumptions? For this discussion, facts are statements of known data and assets available for the mission. Assumptions replace necessary but missing or unknown facts.

    Assumptions must pass two tests. The first test is the validity test. Will this situation still exist when the plan becomes an order? The second test is the necessity test. Is this assumption essential to the solution of the problem? Moreover, will the results of the plan change if we do not make this assumption?

6.  Conduct a risk assessment. What risks are you willing to take in accomplishing this mission? What are the risks to the organization if we do not solve this problem?

7.  Plan for use of available time. Keep in mind that subordinate organizations need time to do the same analysis at their levels.

8.  Issue a restated mission based on the analysis of the problem.

9.  Develop the initial commander's (boss') intent. Identify the key tasks. The key tasks are those tasks that must be performed or the conditions that must

be met to achieve the stated purpose or solve the problem. Key tasks are those tasks or processes that are fundamental to the organization's success. The initial intent should also include the desired end state or destination situation after solving the problem.

10. Issue the guidance to the subordinate organizations/sections.

11. Review the facts and assumptions a second time for validity and necessity.

The next step in the decision making model is the course of action development. What are the options for action? Always keep in mind that one potential course of action is to do nothing and hope the problem will go away. This is not usually a viable course of action and could very well be the reason the problem existed to begin with.

During this phase, the following actions take place: Analysis of your capabilities, the generation of options, the development of the scheme of operations, and assigning responsibility for actions. The courses of action that are developed in this phase must meet the following criteria to be considered in subsequent phases of the decision making model:

1. Suitability—does the course of action accomplish the mission and comply with the commander's guidance?

2. Feasibility—does the unit or firm have the capability to accomplish the mission in terms of time, space, and resources?

3. Acceptability—does the cost justify the gain?

4. Distinguishability—does this course of action significantly differ from other courses of action?

5. Completeness—does this course of action answer the questions of Who, What, When, Where, How, and Why?

The next step in the model is the Course of Action Analysis. During this phase of the model is where the concept of "war-gaming" is applied. Staff officers must anticipate events and what the reactions for each action taken. During this "war-gaming" it is imperative that the participants remain objective and not become attached to a particular action or course of action. During the analysis, if any of the courses of action do not pass the feasibility, acceptability, or suitability tests, reject that course of action. You do not make comparisons between courses of action during this phase. The main purpose of this phase is to record all strengths and weaknesses for each course of action.

After analyzing each course of action, it is time to start the course of action comparisons. During this phase of the decision making model the following actions, take place:

- The staff analyzes and evaluates each course of action.

- Highlight the advantages and disadvantages for each course of action.

- Determine which action has highest probability of success.

- Determine which action poses the minimum risk.

- Ascertain which action best positions the force for future operations.

After analyzing and comparing all of the courses of action, the commander (boss/leader) has the necessary information before him/her to make a logical decision and issue the orders for implementation.

As with any methodology, there are criticisms and benefits. The criticisms of the Military Decision Making Process include that it is too rigid, that it is time consuming, too deliberate, and too resource intensive. This process tends to err on the side of caution—the primary reason for this is if a course of action does not work for the military, there will be undue loss of lives. Although the Army does not really consider the financial impacts to the bottom line, the unnecessary loss of lives is too important to risk with faulty analysis and course of action development. In business, the lack of careful analysis and comparison of courses of action may well result in the loss of a business.

This same model can be applied to various supply chain problems such as deciding on the location of a new distribution center, or even if a new distribution center is necessary. The model can be used to determine if a new Warehousing Management System is necessary and if so, which one. Another potential use of this model for supply chains is the selection of a Third Party Provider or keeping the function in house.

Whatever the application, the Military Decision Making Process model provides the user with a simple to use, easy to understand model that has multiple applications to supply chain management. The Military Decision Making Process is also applicable for solving personal problems such as planning on where to go on vacation this year to meet the needs of everyone in the family. The model will not make the decision for you but it will guide you to making a logical decision if the steps are followed and the questions for each step are answered in an unbiased manner.

Let us look at using the model to determine the location or need for a new distribution center:

1.  Receipt of the Mission—This is determined to be guidance from the boss to look at the capability of the current distribution center to meet the needs of growth and customer support.

2.  Mission Analysis—what is the implied mission and the stated mission? Does the boss want a new distribution center, a larger distribution center, or does he want us to look at outsourcing the operations all together?

3.  Course of Action Development—what are the feasible, suitable, and acceptable courses of action? The possible courses of action based on what we have from the boss could include:

    • Do nothing—this is the status quo, tell the boss that the current center will work and drive on. This may not meet the intent of what the boss is looking for and will take a good deal of data to back it up.

    • Build a new distribution center. Grainger choose this option in Mira Loma, California. Their rationale was that by building a new facility, they could design it to meet their needs and growth plans. This is the same decision that Target reached in their plan to expand the number of distribution centers rather than expand the old ones.

    • Take over an old/abandoned distribution center. Amazon.com choose this option for their Kansas distribution center. Amazingly, this option is not always the preferred option. This is evident by the "new" state of the art facility in Hesperia, California. In 1997, Heilig-Myers built a new facility in Hesperia, only to go bankrupt and out of business within two years. This left the new facility vacant in a close vicinity to several major transportation corridors. As of this writing, that facility is still vacant.

    • Outsource to a Third Party Logistics Provider (3PL). This option is a popular option when companies realize that storage and distribution is not one of their core competencies.

    • Expand the current distribution center in size and/or in technology. This option could include actual construction to the facility, implementing new technologies to expedite the flow of material through the center, or adding a mezzanine to increase the storage capability.

4.   Course of Action Analysis. What is the most feasible, suitable, and accept-able solution? This analysis could be as simple as constructing a matrix of the important criteria to meet the intent of the boss. The matrix could be as sim-ple as:

| COA/ Success criteria | Cost | ROI | Improve Customer Satisfaction | Posture for future operations |
|---|---|---|---|---|
| Build | | | | |
| Take existing DC | | | | |
| Expand | | | | |
| Outsource | | | | |
| Do Nothing | | | | |

Figure 4. Course of Action Analysis

5.   Course of Action Comparison. Determine which of the courses of action meet the boss' intent and meet the majority (preferably all) of the identified success criteria.

6.   Course of Action Approval.

A personal use of the model could be determining where to go on the family vacation this year. The use of the model for this purpose would look something like this:

1.   Mission. A vacation that the entire family will enjoy.

2.   Mission Analysis. The family's guidance is that it must be affordable, every-one goes, and there is something for everyone in the family to do (this part gets more difficult the older the children become). The success criteria according to the family members are that there must be golf, shopping, and a beach or good swimming pool.

3.   Courses of Action. The courses of action that meets the above success criteria are Hawaii, Palm Springs, Las Vegas, Orlando, and a visit to the relatives.

4.  Analysis. Unless your relatives are rich and live in one of the other alternative locations, I would submit to you that this is not a viable course of action. A visit to the relatives is an obligation, not a vacation.

5.  Comparison. Which of the courses of action meet the most of the success criteria? This will really depend on the time of year that you are planning a vacation. If it were summer time obviously, Las Vegas and Palm Springs would be cheaper, as long as you can handle the heat outside—this may put an unacceptable mark beside the golf criterion.

6.  Decision. This one is a personal decision for your family. I will not get into the travel recommendations during this discussion.

The Military Decision Making Process is a useful tool to plan major military operation, a successful expansion operation, or even a family vacation destination. The steps of the model will guide you in your decision-making. This model will not make the decision for you. In the case of a business decision, it will guide you to the best solution. However, professional judgment is still required and a bit of salesmanship may be necessary if the logical decision is not the one previously thought to be the best one.

# 5

# *Applying Six-sigma to Your Supply Chain*

o o o o o o o o o o o o o o o o o o o o o o o o o o o o o o o o o o o o
*"Six-sigma produces a realization that processes do not start and stop at the doors or walls of your organization."*

—*Jim McNerney, CEO of 3M*

The US Army's customer order cycle times in 1995 within the Continental United States was more than four times that of the North Korean Army in 1951. This chapter uses the US Army as the case study to demonstrate the potential benefits of applying a Six-sigma methodology to supply chain operations and how to apply the methodology to achieve results.

## *Background on Six-sigma*

What is six-sigma? Literally, six-sigma is a statistical measurement of plus or minus six standard deviations from the centerline of the distribution in a control chart. Statistically speaking, six-sigma can be interpreted as 3.2 errors per one million opportunities.[1]

For the discussions in this chapter, six-sigma will refer to a business process that is focused on the customer, a process that looks at the minimization of waste and process variation to improve customer service. After all, if a process does not

---

1.  The one million opportunities could be one million items produced, one million documents processed, or one million orders processed. The measurement is not as important as the process of getting as close to one hundred percent accuracy. Although sometimes difficult to achieve, the customer expects it every time.

meet customer expectations or add value to the company, why would you want to do it?

Why should you want to look at six-sigma for your supply chain operations? Six-sigma uses metrics to calculate the success of everything an organization does. It provides a methodology to question every process and every step in an organization or supply chain and it uses analytical tools to pinpoint sources of errors and identifies ways to eliminate them. The real reason is that six-sigma is a proven way to influence the bottom line while improving customer service.

Before we look at how to apply six-sigma to your supply chain let us look at what six-sigma is not. Six-sigma is not a management fad. Fortune Magazine featured an article in the January 22, 2001 edition titled "Why You Can Safely Ignore Six Sigma." In this article, the author explained that six-sigma is the latest management fad and would pass like other fads. Other fads that have come and gone fit into the "flavor of the month" category. These fads crop up on a regular basis because some business guru publishes a book or article detailing the fad and everyone joins the cause.

Another example of the misunderstanding of six-sigma as a tool for process improvement and process variation reduction appeared in the APICS *2000 International Conference Proceedings.* In a article titled "Speed Up Your Lean Implementation with TOC," John Saathoff wrote, "Commonly observed behaviors include put the organization on the 'program of the year'—reengineering, six sigma, high performance work teams, etc." Where it is true that most "programs of the year" such as reengineering were not successful, numerous companies have achieved success with six-sigma. The confusion comes when folks try to implement a six-sigma quality program without knowing what the processes are that they are trying to improve. In the same paper, Mr. Saathoff quotes the Harris Corporation as saying "we're unique." My experience tells me that although every corporation is "unique," when management states they are unique they are really saying we do not want to change.

Although six-sigma, Just-in-Time, and the Theory of Constraints are different programs, a careful look at the result of these programs reveals that they are very similar in nature. Six-sigma quality programs, Just-in-Time inventory management programs, and the Theory of Constraints all seek to eliminate non-value-added processes and procedures.

Six-sigma started gaining notoriety in the 1980s with its successful and highly publicized implementation at Motorola. General Electric adopted the methodology and the accompanying focus on customer support and reducing process variation. The use of six-sigma by General Electric has received more publicity than the adoption by other companies such as Honeywell. The leadership emphasis within General Electric contributed to the publicity. Part of the continued popularity of six-sigma can be attributed to the leaders of General Electric that have moved on to other companies such as Honeywell, 3M and The Home Depot.

Jack Welch, former CEO of General Electric, went as far as putting six-sigma improvement goals in the company's annual report and mentioned the goals in the annual shareholders meetings. He is credited with exporting the success of six-sigma to all subsidiaries of General Electric and told shareholders that six-sigma was credited with millions of dollars in annual cost savings and in improving product quality.

## *Methodology for Applying Six-sigma*

Motorola implemented a six step program for six-sigma. The steps of the Motorola approach are:

1. Identify the product you create or the service you provide.

2. Identify your customers and what is important to them.

3. Identify what you need to provide the product or service that satisfies customers.

4. Define the process for doing the work.

5. Mistake proof the process and eliminate wasted effort.

6. Ensure continuous improvement by measuring, analyzing, and controlling the improved process.

The General Electric approach is similar in nature but only contains five steps:

1. **Define**

2. **Measure**

3. **Analyze**

4. **Improve**

5. **Control**

In 1995, the US Army implemented a test program known then as Velocity Management that was a six-sigma like program. This program started as a test program at key Army installations. The purpose was to determine the viability of the concepts to military supply chain issues. The program was then expanded to an Army wide program and later spilled over to the other services and the Department of Defense. The Army's program used what I call simplified six-sigma and only contained three steps. Most of the elements of the six steps of Motorola and the five steps of the GE DMAIC concept are in these three steps. The Army's three steps were simply:

1. **D**efine

2. **M**easure

3. **I**mprove

Essential to the Army's approach was the support of senior leaders throughout the Army. The results of the successful implementations at the test locations convinced the senior leaders of the viability of the program. Armed with the results in reducing Order Ship Times[2] at these key locations and then the success of the Army wide implementation, the Army expanded the Velocity Management Program to other links of the supply chain. Using six-sigma techniques the Army was able to achieve reductions of Order Ship Times and later Actual Customer Wait Times[3] of over four hundred percent.

The key to achieving the goals of your quality improvement program is first to define your processes. The best way to define your processes is physically walking the process. All too often managers believe that they can manage processes from behind a computer screen. Managers believe that they can find all of the data nec-

---

2.   This segment of the supply chain was chosen because data for this segment had been captured for over twenty years and therefore establishing a baseline for measuring improvements was easy to accomplish without creating a need for additional data collection. This measurement was a subset of what is now Customer Wait Time. The commercial equivalent of the Army's Order Ship Times is Customer Order Cycle Times.

3.   The Army defined Customer Wait Time as the total amount of time from the identification of the need for an item until it is in the hands of the ultimate customer. For example if a part is needed for a vehicle, the Customer Wait Time would be the time necessary for the part to be ordered through the supply chain and back to the mechanic that ordered the part. For the Army's National Training Center, Customer Wait Times were reduced from 28+ days to 4.6 days.

essary to make decisions and determine how things really operate on the computer.

To know what is really going on in a process, you have to walk the process yourself. Dr. W. Edwards Deming on many occasions told seminar and lecture groups, "If you can't describe what you are doing as a process, you don't know what you are doing." Michael Dell takes it a step farther by saying, "Until you look inside and understand what's going on by business, by customer, and by geography, you don't know anything." Are you starting to get the point that it is important to know your processes? Sun Tzu reminds us that we have to get down on the ground to get the perspective of the soldier. General Robert E. Lee called this doing your on reconnaissance. The same is true in supply chains—we have to get down on the ground to get the perspective of the workers to know how the process actually works.

Part of defining the process is defining who your customers are. What do they want from you and what are your capabilities to provide the goods or services that they desire.

As you walk the process, it is important to document every action and record the times of rest, movement, processing, queue, and in-transit times. While you are walking the process you have to take the time to ask the workers what they are doing and why. The responses will sometimes amaze you. What we discovered in the Army was that the actual steps and processes, not to mention times, were much different from what the managers briefed to us before the process walk.

As you ask why, the key is to be genuinely interested in why the workers are doing something and why they are doing it that way. Avoid asking why in a condescending way. This form of questioning will only alienate the workers. What you will find out is that in many cases the "why" fits into several sacred cow categories:

1.   "We have always done it that way."

2.   "The regulation states......"

3.   "This is the way I was taught to do it."

By walking the process, we discovered that it was taking as long to process electrons in the computer systems as it took to process the actual material through the distribution system.

The most interesting revelation was sacred cow category number three. We discovered that we had perpetuated an antiquated system and had in fact been teaching wrong methods in the school systems. One of the senior supply technicians brought everything into perspective when it exclaimed, "we did it wrong for so long that wrong looked right." As you walk the process and document what your as-is situation is, ask yourself if your company is in the same boat of "doing it wrong so long that wrong" looks right.

Once you document the process in a detailed process map,[4] the next critical step is to establish goals for improving the supply chain and establishing measures or metrics to track the improvements.

A critical lesson that we learned in the Army in setting goals is that a "one-size fits all goal" for the organization may not be appropriate. Although the Army is indeed an "Army of One," the Army is composed of three distinct components: The Active Army, the US Army Reserve, and the Army National Guard. Initially a standard goal for improvement for the total Army was established. What we did not take into account (and in fact it took two years to realize) was that the Army Reserve and the National Guard units saw the goals for the Active Army as unreachable. Therefore, the Active Army made great gains in supply chain improvements while the Reserve components actually digressed in performance. We established separate goals for the Active Army and the Reserve components once we realized what the single goal was doing to the Reserve Components. Within six months of establishing an "achievable" goal, the Reserve components exceeded their improvement goals for the year. Make sure the workers perceive the goals as achievable, if not, they will not buy into them and will not work to meet them.

Focus on the customer as you start setting goals for improvement in your supply chain and working on measures of success. Remember if the measure is not important to improving customer support or meeting the needs of the customer, you may be measuring the wrong things. Do not let pride influence what you measure. Some companies want to measure and report what they do well but not what affects the customer. If you think you are doing great in meeting the customers' needs in your supply chain but the customer does not you need to take a close look at what you are measuring.

The measurements will provide your organization with a common language for tracking improvements. In addition, they give you solid information. Every operation has perceptions, intuition, and reality. Management has their perception of how operations are functioning. Measurements are necessary to focus the

---

4.   A process map is nothing more than a flow chart of all the actions within a process or within the supply chain.

efforts to reduce the delta between the perceptions, intuitions on how well we are responding to the customer, and the reality of what is going on in your supply chain. Once the metrics or measures are established, a baseline will serve as the yardstick for measuring improvements. It is important to have one baseline for the entire period of the six-sigma project. Some companies change their baseline every year to show current improvements or to "pad" the progress of improvement. Avoid the temptation to change the baseline just to look better.

Once the measures are in place, it is time to start moving from the as-is situation to the destination situation using the measures as the bridge to get there. The process map will identify those processes that are quick fixes (sometimes called low hanging fruit) and those processes that may take a little longer to fix (stretch goals). The processes that take longer to fix usually fit into the sacred cow category of "we've always done it that way."

The next critical step in the six-sigma improvement cycle is to document the changes, then go back, and walk the process again. The routine walking of the process ensures that new problem areas identification, ensures that one fix did not create a new problem, and keeps the workers and the leaders fresh while ensuring continuous improvement.

## Benchmarking against "World Class Operations"

Benchmarking your supply chain against world class or best of breed companies is critical to the success of your program and your supply chain. All too often companies only want to benchmark against the competition. Sometimes the competition is not the best of breed to begin with either. In this case, you may find the benchmark may be outside of your normal operational environment. However, even if you are not benchmarking against your direct competition, you still need to know how they are doing business so you can gain a competitive advantage in supporting your customers.

The classic example of looking outside your area for benchmarking operations took place within Southwest Airlines. Southwest determined that the way to be success and profitable was to have as many seats filled on as many flights every day. They reasoned that a plane sitting on the tarmac is not making money for the company. As they looked for a benchmark, they looked at the pit stop operations of NASCAR. This benchmarking enabled them to establish procedures to more quickly prepare planes for the next flight and reduce the on the ground time for aircraft.

# Results for the Army

The first real benefit from implementing six-sigma concepts for the Army was a move away from measures that focused on individual links in the supply chain to customer centric measures. The initial measures of the links in the supply chain were captured in an outdated report known as the Independent Direct Support Activity Processing Report. This report measured how well each link in the chain performed but did not measure the actual time for the soldier to get his/her part or item of supply. The new metric, Customer Wait Time, focuses on the actual time necessary from the identification of a need until the soldier has the part he/she needs to fix a vehicle or has the item of supply needed in hand.

The next benefit for the Army from six-sigma was a new focus on what supplies should be stocked in what locations based on the usage by the units in the field. When the Army first implemented the Velocity Management Program, over sixty percent of all parts delivered to Fort Irwin, California (in the middle of the Mojave Desert), were being shipped from an east coast distribution center. The Defense Logistics Agency maintained a mirror-image distribution center eight hours away in Stockton, California. Logic would suggest that parts coming to the National Training Center from a California distribution center would arrive quicker than supplies coming from the other side of the country. Similarly an equal number of parts going to Europe were being shipped from Stockton, California, rather than coming out of the distribution center in Pennsylvania. Since no one was tracking who was filling what requisitions, no one really knew the impacts of the stockage policies. The policy provided incentives to the buyers to have shipments from vendors delivered to the distribution center closest to the supplier. Reduced transportation costs from the vendors served as the rationale for this policy. The actuality was that this policy was costing more money in supply chain costs because of additional secondary transportation and handling costs.

We have already discussed the up to four hundred percent reductions in Customer Wait Times. The fallout of the reduced wait time was a reduction across the Army in the depth of the local storage sites and an accompanying increase in the number of SKUs[5] stocked at the local warehouses. The reduced wait times coupled with the greater availability of local supplies from the increased SKUs resulted in a fifty percent reduction in maintenance processing times. The main-

---

5.    SKU: Stock-Keeping Units. An item of inventory in a warehouse or distribution center.

tenance processing times coupled with the reduced stockage levels provided cost savings of greater than three hundred million dollars over a two-year period. These savings came from an investment of less than one million dollars over the same two years. This is not a bad Return on Investment for the Army or the tax-payer. Similar results are possible in your operation. No "flavor of the month" fad will give you results of this kind. Results like these not only make the customers happy but also the stockholders.

## *Conclusions*

Six-sigma is not a fad or "flavor of the month" business initiative. It is a cus-tomer-focused approach to improving quality and reducing process variations. It is a simple to understand and simple to implement improvement process, as long as the senior leadership of the company buys into it and serves as the six-sigma champions as Jack Welch did for General Electric. One of the by-products of six-sigma is the process map. This tool is not only good for identifying areas needing improvement, but it is also a great tool for training new employees on the pro-cesses within your company.

# 6

# *Change Management—Using the Power of Change in Today's Environment for Your Supply Chain*

*The greatest challenge to individuals, organizations, and society itself will be the ability to cope with an ever-increasing rate of change in technology and human behavior."*

—Alvin Tofler, Future Shock, 1971

The last chapter looked at the use of six-sigma to improve supply chain processes. In this chapter, we will look at how to use change and how to harness the power of change in light of today's economic environment. In the course of this discussion, we will look at how to influence and lead change. You can depend on one constant. Things will change. As a leader, you have the choice of influencing that change or you can be a not so innocent bystander.

*"Every improvement is change but not every change is an improvement!"*

All to often people assume that any change is good and must be an improvement. How many managers have you seen come in and want to change just for the sake of change with the philosophy that change gives the illusion of progress? All too often, this happens. Unfortunately, for many firms, the Army included; managers on the "fast track" move before the impacts of such needless changes are really felt by the organization. The new manager receives the blame for the poor performance resulting from the change. For this reason, we will focus on

69

improvements in this chapter and not just change. The study of change and improvements has produced some of the best selling business books of all time. Let us look at some of the books that fit that category:

1.  Peters' and Waterman's classic from the 1980s—*In Search of Excellence.*

2.  Tom Peters' follow on classic *Thriving on Chaos.*

3.  Dr. Eli Goldratt's *The Goal*—which opened the eyes of the business and logistics worlds to the Theory of Constraints.

4.  The faddish books of the early 1990s—*Reengineering the Corporation* and *Reengineering Management.*

5.  The classic *Teaching the Elephants to Dance.*

6.  Blanchard and Johnson's *Gung Ho.*

7.  Dr. Kreigle's *Sacred Cows Make the Best Burgers* and *If It Ain't Broke, Break It!*

8.  Dr. Johnson's most recent classic—*Who Moved My Cheese?*

9.  Dr. Jim Tomkins' recent book *Revolution.*

> *"Some people have the ability to look at change as an opportunity to succeed, while others look at change as putting them at risk to fail."*
>
> *—Mark Schroeder, DSC Logistics*
> *Senior Vice President, Operations*

Obviously not enough people comprehended these books or ignored them as we moved into the twenty-first century. Just look at the problems that resulting from the actions of Enron, Global Crossing, WorldCom, and K-Mart. The lessons of the new century are change or have change forced upon you. Very often, the alternative to change (improvement changes) is business failure. Consider the statement made in the Modern Materials Handling Early Edition on February 26, 2002: "At a recent Council of Logistics Management seminar, all of the 300 attendees raised their hands when asked if they were involved in a major corporate change initiative. When asked if they were satisfied with the results of those changes, not one person raised a hand." Why were they not satisfied? Could it be that again change has been mistaken for improvement and since the change did not bring improvement, the attendees were therefore disappointed? On the other hand, could it be that no one was leading the change?

Before we get into the answers to these questions, it is time to look at some of the headlines dealing with change that shaped the economic environment in the past several years.

1. *Los Angeles Times,* January 29, 2002—"Toys R Us to Cut Jobs, Close 64 US Stores."

2. *Los Angeles Times,* January 23, 2002—"K-Mart Seeks Bankruptcy Protection, Amazon.com Reports its First Profits."

3. *Florida Today,* January 12, 2002—"Ford to Slash 35,000 Jobs, 5 Plants."

4. *USA Today,* March 11, 2002—"248 Businesses to Declare Chapter 11 This Year."

5. *Orlando Sentinel,* March 11, 2002—"K-Mart to Close 284 Under Performing Stores."

6. *Logistics Management Website,* January 2002—"A study released Friday (January 11) predicts the Sep 11 terrorist attackers will reverberate through the US economy for years wiping out more that 1.6 million jobs in 2002 alone…already 248,000jobs have been lost because of the attacks."

A variety of perils for the first years of the twenty first century: major retailers declaring bankruptcy, large automobile manufacturers closing plants and laying off thousands of employees, closing of stores, and loss of jobs. Change is happening all around us and it appears that most of the changes are not improvements.

Champions of harnessing change for improvements include media giant FOX. When FOX first came along it was just another of the minor networks trying to make a name. Then FOX grasped the need to find a way to break out of the pack of also-rans. Now FOX has the game of the week in Baseball, National Football League games, and NASCAR for half of each racing season. In addition, FOX News provided the best coverage of the action in Operation Iraqi Freedom (at least from the perspective of this participant).

Another champion of improving and changing is Madonna. Madonna has been around as a top performer for over twenty years. Why? She has constantly changed her image and her music to match the needs of the music buying public. She is as popular today with my daughters as she was with others in the 1980s.

The Bee Gees did the same thing in the 1970s, took advantage of the "Disco" craze, and significantly extended their music career.

Wal-Mart is another champion of change. As they identify needs of the customer that other retailers are not meeting successfully, Wal-Mart moves into that area. Their superstore concept of a retailer and a grocery store in one store continues to win customers away from the competition.

The other side of the champions of change includes previous stalwarts such as Sunbeam, K-Mart, Home Quarters, and Hechinger's. Growing up and in my early career the most common kitchen appliance was Sunbeam. Looking back it was almost as common as an appliance from Sears is in today's kitchens. Today Sunbeam is gone. This once prominent company became a victim of poor leadership and an apparent unwillingness to change.

K-Mart, as detailed in some of the articles listed above, went from the top discount retailer in the nation to bankruptcy because they did not change to meet the needs of the consumer and they were outflanked by Wal-Mart. A worse fate befell Home Quarters, Hechinger's, and Home Owners' Warehouse. All of these home improvement warehouses have fallen by the wayside and no longer exist because they did not change their methods to compete with The Home Depot.

What can leadership do to harness and direct the inevitable change process? Leaders are responsible for causing change in their organization; leading the change; providing focus to the change processes; and managing the change process.

The first step is to identify what needs to be improved. Again, remember do not just change for the sake of change. You have to pinpoint the core problem or the areas that need improvement. The best way to identify these problem areas is to physically walk the process and ask what is going on and why.

Once the company identifies the areas in need of changing, the leadership team has to establish the vision to focus the change. The vision has to be communicated, concise, and most importantly, understood by the employees. Cute slogans are nice but without a communicated and understood vision, the change will not be an improvement.

The next step is to develop a written implementation plan. The written plan serves as the vehicle to communicate to employees, shareholders, and customers the vision. It also serves to enforce the leader's support and commitment to the change process. Studies show that greater than seventy-five percent of all process improvement programs fail. The most common reason for the failures is the lack of leadership involvement and support for the project. The written implementation plan and the vision establish the leadership as the sponsors of the change.

Once a plan is in place, the use of multifunctional teams brings a wider experience level to the table and gets more departments to buy into the process early on. In the Army's Velocity Management Program, we employed a combination of a Process Improvement Teams at the corporate level. These teams of subject matter experts from across the supply chain focused the efforts of the Site Improvement Teams at each installation. The Process Improvement Teams moderated and facilitated changes. These teams visited every major installation to provide education and training to the Site Improvement Teams.

The Site Improvement Teams were composed of the local supply chain experts and customers of the supply chain. The local teams routinely walked the processes at their installation to identify problem areas and established the priorities for the local improvement programs.

The improvement process starts with the identification of the root cause of a problem and the publishing of the leadership vision for the future. The understanding of how the process will work then accelerates the process. The written implementation plan moves the program forward and when coupled with the proper resources, commitment of the workers, education for all those involved, and dedication produce a successful improvement program.

There are several important obstacles to every improvement program. It always takes longer than you think it should; no project is ever as easy as it appears on paper; and until employees are convinced of "what's in it for me?" they will procrastinate and slow down the project. There are other areas of resistance to watch for:

- Human nature provides an inherent resistance to change and resistance to leaving a comfort zone.

- Change produces a concern over job protection (more of "what's in it for me?"). A commonly encountered concern is "if I do it better and faster, I may be out of a job." How many of you can honestly say that you have too many employees in your distribution center?

- A common roadblock to change is a case of "not invented here" syndrome. All too often, this kills a good idea. There are a certain percentage of employees and managers that seem to feel like if they did not think of it, it must not be a good idea

- An important lesson we learned in the Army is that without a formal process to stimulate the improvement it will not happen.

Change in an organization is inevitable, as a leader your choice is to lead the change and harness its energy to make your organization better or let the process lead you. The choice is yours. I like to remind people that they need to remember the "dead fish." Remember, even a dead fish can swim downstream and give the illusion of progress! Swimming against the current can be difficult but the rewards are worth the effort.

# 7

# *Process Improvement Methodologies*

*"In baseball and in life, your condition, confidence, and concentration affect your performance. There's mistakes-and there's wrong mistakes."*

*—Yogi Berra*

The purpose of process improvement programs is to ensure that you are not making the "wrong mistakes." In this chapter, we will look at the most successful process improvement programs and the methodologies for applying them to improving your supply chain.

As a young Reserve Officers Training Course (ROTC) cadet at North Carolina State University, I had one instructor and advisor to our military fraternity that told us there were only a few ways to solve problems. Major Baucomm told us you could take action, wait and see if others would take action, or do nothing and hope the problem goes away. I have since learned that waiting for someone else to solve the problem or doing nothing and hoping the problem would go away are not viable courses of action. I have also learned that Albert Einstein was correct when he stated, "The significant problems we face cannot be solved at the same level of thinking we were at when we created them."

What is process improvement? It is a methodology for fixing problems while leaving the basic structures in place. It is a way to develop focused solutions to eliminate the root causes of problems and not just treating the symptoms. Process improvement should not be confused with process redesign or reengineering. Redesign and reengineering focus on replacing the process with a new one all-together rather than simply fixing the original problem. These two methods usually employ the use of incremental changes.

Why improve? Alvin Tofler tells us we have to improve our processes or be left behind in a state of shock wondering what happened. In most cases in today's business environment, it is a situation of change or be changed. For the Army that was the option we faced in 1995. The Cold War was over; the Army's logistics structure was patterned after the Cold War model in spite of the successes of a modified logistics system during the Gulf War. Customer wait times were in some cases as long as one hundred and twenty-two days for critical repair parts and there were no formal systems in place to make improvements to the system. Other companies have faced or will soon face the same ultimatum from their customers and shareholders—change to support the customer, face forced change, or go the way of the Mojave Desert Tortoise and face extinction.

If we accept that change is inevitable and that what we really want to do is improve the processes and not just change them (as discussed in chapter 5), then it is important to look at those process improvement methodologies that will give us the most "bang for the buck."

In this chapter, we will look at the methodologies used at the Army's National Training Center to reduce Customer Wait Times by over fifty percent in one year. These methods produced significant man-hour reductions, improved customer service, and enabled us to realize real dollar savings of $4.9 million.

The most successful process improvement methods over the past decade have been Just-in-Time (when viewed as a process improvement methodology as opposed to a zero inventory mentality), applications of the Theory of Constraints, and six-sigma. The question we will try to answer in this chapter is are the three methodologies really the same thing with a different name, a logical evolution of thought, or are the three methods distinctly different methodologies?

## *Just-in-Time*

The *APICS Dictionary*[1] defines Just-in-Time as: "a philosophy of manufacturing

---

1.   The 10th Edition of the *APICS Dictionary* is available online for APICS members or available through the APICS Bookstore. This reference book is extremely helpful in establishing definitions for supply chain terms.

based on planned elimination of waste and on continuous improvement of productivity."[2]

When analyzing Just-in-Time it is important to look at it as a way of eliminating waste and improving productivity. All too often, the discussions on Just-in-Time focus on the zero inventory concepts and companies are immediately turned off by the concept and with good reason. Companies that advocated zero inventories were caught short by the longshoreman strike on the west coast of the United States in late 2002 and in the aftermath of the September 11, 2001 attacks. These two incidents started companies to relook the zero inventory mentality.

The first step of a Just-in-Time program is to document the existing flow of products or services. This documentation will enable you to see the actual flow and determine which processes or services are value-added and which ones are simply waste. *Just-in-Time: Making it Happen*[3] lists the following as the seven wastes that Just-in-Time can identify:

1.  The waste of overproduction

2.  The waste of waiting

3.  The waste of transportation

4.  The waste of stocks

5.  The waste of motion

6.  The waste of making defects

7.  The waste of production

The waste of overproduction occurs all too frequently as companies continue to produce in large batches to save a few dollars on production runs. Overproduction also occurs when companies do not accurately forecast sales or usage of an item.

The waste of waiting can come from too much upstream production creating additional queues in front of bottlenecks. A worse form of the waste of waiting

2.  APICS, 2003,
    http://members.apics.org/Publications/dictionary/articles.asp?ID=1648
3.  Sandras, William A., Jr., *Just-in-Time: Making it Happen*, Oliver Wight Publications, Essex, VT, 1989.

comes from poor production planning and inaccurate bills of materials and inaccurate lead times. This ties up dollars in inventory that is sitting, waiting for the rest of the parts to arrive for assembly or production. Walking the process and looking at the queues and wait times can prevent this along with regular reviews of the master production schedule and the supporting bills of materials.

The waste of transportation is a direct result of warehouse layout, distribution planning and optimization of distribution routes. In a distribution center, the majority of a worker's time is moving through the center to get to the location to pick parts. Reorganizing the warehouse or distribution center can reduce this time and save on transportation time. In manufacturing, the use of work cells reduces transportation times and move times within the factory. Closely locating suppliers to the manufacturing plant is another method of reducing transportation time.

Careful distribution and warehousing planning is another method for reducing transportation from the distribution center to the customer, provides a more responsive level of support, and gives the illusion of close to Just-in-Time support to the customer. A major consulting group conducts a study every year based on the population centers of the United States and the major transportation nodes and modes to determine the optimal locations for distribution centers. The study compares the optimal number of centers a corporation desires and the locations of those centers to best serve the entire country. The closer to the major customers and major transportation nodes you place your distribution center the more responsive your support will be.

Another method of reducing transportation time is to locate your distribution centers close to your major suppliers. The rationale for this solution is that the closer your distribution center is to the supplier, the faster you can get your supplies and there is an added benefit of reduced transportation costs passed from the supplier to you.

Just-in-Time looks closely at the waste of stocks. Unfortunately, this area garners the most attention of opponents of Just-in-Time. However, there are some obvious reasons for not carrying excess stocks. By excess, I am referring to those stocks that exceed your normal operating levels. The Department of Defense learned that carrying excess stocks for weapon systems created a multitude of problems. As more modern systems and equipment comes in to the military forces, the stocks on the shelves for the older systems becomes obsolete. As equipment that is more modern is available, the demand for the older parts, even from the Foreign Military Sales Program, dries up. By the late 1990s, the Department of Defense found themselves with billions of dollars of obsolete parts for systems that were no longer in use. Could this have been prevented? Of course, it could. As systems are designed and tested for future use, the procurement of new parts for the old systems should be reduced or halted. The key here to preventing this is communication between the research and development people, the acquisition offices and the supply chain personnel.

The waste of stocks also extends to the costs of pilferage, the costs of damage within the warehouse, and the cost of storage of the items. We sometimes overlook another cost of maintaining excess stocks. This cost is the contribution of excess stocks to the waste of transportation and motion within the distribution center. One defense distribution center with a large amount of excess and obsolete stocks (they called them dormant because no one had ordered them in over two years. I call that obsolete) had workers walking past the "dormant" stocks to get to the active stocks on a regular basis. This increased the movement time to get to locations to pick orders.

The waste of motion is simply moving stuff more than necessary. During Operation Iraqi Freedom, we violated this principle. Often the violation of this principle can be traced to metrics that promote suboptimizing supply chain actions. In the case of Operation Iraqi Freedom, the majority of the supplies were transported to Kuwait on a combination of military and contracted civilian aircraft. The supplies were quickly moved off the flight line after being offloaded. The quick movement off the flight line was a security measure but it also expedited to meet the time metrics of the flight line. The supplies were then loaded on a truck and moved to the staging area less than a half-mile away. At this point, the trucks were unloaded and the supplies staged for movement. The supplies were then loaded on another truck and moved to the Theater Distribution Center about thirty minutes away. If trucks were not available or if the supplies were not properly packed, the trucks were again unloaded, the supplies repacked and staged in a customer-shipping lane until the outbound trucks arrived. The outgoing supplies were once again loaded on trucks and moved to the customers. On the days that the supplies were properly packed and trucks were on time, cross docking was a reality. This significantly reduced the amount of handling.

How the supplies coming into Kuwait were packed also contributed to the waste of motion. The Department of Defense is tied to the archaic concept of shipping supplies in a tri-wall "multi-pack" box. This box is the size of a standard warehouse pallet and approximately three feet high. The consolidation of multiple orders into one "multi-pack" contributes to maximizing shipment loads. However, if the "multi-pack" has items for multiple consignees in the same box, an additional sort is required to put the proper items in the proper customer locations. This solution to this situation is simple. Get away from the large multi-pack concept and adopt a smaller shipping container. Grainger uses a much smaller box to ship to customers and can arrange multiple customer boxes on the same pallet without commingling the customer orders into the same box.

The biggest focus of process improvement programs such as Just-in-Time is the reduction of the waste of producing defective items. Inspection after the fact will not eliminate or reduce this waste. The quality has to be built in to the product or service. In distribution, the waste of producing defective items comes from shipping the defective item or just as bad shipping the wrong item to the customer. It does no good to the company or the customer to streamline the times to deliver supplies if we send them the wrong items.

The final waste of over production also affects the supply chain. When manufacturing over produces because their metrics award them for producing large lots and fewer product line change overs, the supply chain gets saddled with where and how to stock the items. Moreover, in some cases, we are back to the problem of obsolete items on the shelf long after the supported product or equipment is no longer in service.

With proper implementation along with support from senior leaders of the organization, Just-in-Time will reduce the inventory on the shelves and in the supply chain because of eliminating the non-value-added and wasteful practices of the company. When viewed simply as an inventory reduction model, Just-in-Time will reduce inventory on the shelves but maybe not the right inventory. This will still leave the inefficient processes in place, thereby creating new and potentially bigger problems in the supply chain.

## *The Theory of Constraints*

*"The Theory of Constraints is a management philosophy that can be viewed as three separate but interrelated areas—logistics, performance measurement, and logical thinking."*

In his book *The Theory of Constraints*[4], Dr. Eli Goldratt lists the following steps in applying the Theory of Constraints (TOC):

---

4.    Goldratt, Elihu, *The Theory of Constraints*, The North River Press Publishing Corporation, Great Barrington, MA, 1990. Dr. Goldratt has several books that discuss the application of the Theory of Constraints to include *The Goal* and *It's Not Luck*. *The Goal* is a great introduction to the principles of the Theory of Constraints.

1. Identify the system's constraints.

2. Decide how to exploit the system's constraints.

3. Subordinate everything else to the above decision.

4. Elevate the system's constraints.

5. If a constraint has been broken, go back to step one, but do not allow inertia to cause a system constraint.

Let us look at these steps in light of producing improvements in supply chain operations. Step one is to identify the system's constraints. How do we do that? In some cases, the constraints are so obvious that very little effort will identify them. In other cases, the best way to identify the constraints is to walk the process. As you walk the process, you will be able to discover where the constraints are in the system and what the impacts of those constraints are. You may discover that there are multiple constraints in which case you have to determine through walking the process which constraint is the major constraint that is causing the greatest impact on efficiency of your supply chain. Focus on one constraint at a time.

The next step is to decide how to attack the problem. This includes focusing all improvement efforts on fixing this constraint on the system. During Operation Iraqi Freedom, the major constraint on the distribution system was transportation assets. The solution was a careful and detailed allocation of transportation assets to ensure as many critical supplies as possible were delivered to the forward units. Every distribution effort was subordinated to this process. The process was elevated to the right level and the appropriate measures put into place to ensure that critical supplies were shipped first and then everything else was shipped as required.

The final step to implementing the Theory of Constraints is the one step that many organizations forget or bypass. The final step is to go back to step one after one constraint has been fixed to identify the new constraint and make sure that the previous success does not create another new constraint. There is always a constraint—when one is eliminated another one will be there. The critical step is to continue walking the process to find the next constraint. This step separates TOC from a reengineering program; it is a continuous process improvement methodology.

# *Six-Sigma*

Although we covered six-sigma in a previous chapter, here we want to look at the similarities or differences between six-sigma and other process improvement methodologies. A flyer from Smarter Solutions states: "As it's practiced today, six-sigma is a methodology for pursuing continuous improvement in customer satisfaction and profit that goes beyond defect reduction and emphasizes business process improvement in general." We will focus on in this section the process improvement aspects. Therefore, let us take another look at the steps used by General Electric, Honeywell, Home Depot, and Penske:

- Define the process

- Measure the process

- Analyze for variations in the process

- Improve the process

- Control the process

Defining the process is very similar in nature to the Theory of Constraints step of identifying the constraint and Just-in-Time step of documenting the flow of products or services to determine if there is value-added.

Measuring and analyzing the process for variations is closely related to the Just-in-Time step of determining the reasons for the variations and the TOC step of decide how to exploit the constraint.

Improving the process in the six-sigma methodology is very similar to the Just-in-Time step of implementing the changes. The final step for all three methodologies is to go back to step one.

In a recent presentation to the World Supply Chain Summit, I showed this slide to compare the three methodologies' main points:

# What is the Difference Between TOC/6 Sigma/JIT?

| Just in Time | Theory of Constraints | Six Sigma |
|---|---|---|
| Document existing flow | Identify the system's constraints | Define the process |
| Determine the reasons for the variation | Decide how to exploit the constraints | Measure the process |
| Implement changes | Subordinate everything else to this decision | Analyze the process |
| Mistake proof system | Elevate constraints | Improve the process |
| Go back to step 1 | Go back to step 1 | Control the process/iterate for continuous improvement |

Figure 5. A comparison of the three process improvement methodologies.

Which of the three methodologies are the best to bring about change in your organization? The DMAIC process of six-sigma combines the best of Just-in-Time and the Theory of Constraints into one easy to apply methodology for holistically looking at your supply chain and improving the processes while improving customer service and support. Six-sigma focuses on the customer and if we do not focus on the customer some one else will.

# 8

## *Qualities of a World Class Distribution Center*

In this chapter, we will look at those qualities that make a distribution center world class. We will look at eighteen qualities or attributes. Your distribution center or warehouse does not need to meet every one of these attributes. However, the more of them that you do meet the better the service you can provide to your customer. The better you meet the needs of the customer, the better your chances of increasing your customer base.

The first attribute is inventory accuracy. The Army used to have a standard of ninety-percent accuracy as the measure of a quality warehouse. Why is this not a good measure of efficiency in a warehouse? In the private sector, ninety-percent inventory accuracy means at least a ten percent-unplanned stock out. Unless you are stocking to one hundred percent of your customers' demands, this ten percent unplanned stock out is probably the little extra frustration that will lead your customers to your competition. In the military, such low inventory accuracy could be the difference between life and death of a soldier. In addition to the customer frustration, you need to calculate the financial shortfall from not having ten percent of your valuable inventory on the shelf. **The inventory accuracy standard for world class is one hundred percent.**

The next attribute is **perfect order fulfillment.** This relates to the inventory accuracy and to stocking the right items on the shelf. Perfect order fulfillment is a combination of having the right items in the distribution center and picking and packing the right quantity to meet the customer demand. Again, just like inventory accuracy the standard is one hundred percent.

**Value added services.** What services beyond just picking and packing are you providing your customers? Are they asking for custom shipping labels, custom packaging? Are you providing it for them? If you are not, I can assure you that someone else will and your customer will walk.

**Distribution center cleanliness.** Every world class distribution center and warehouse that I have been in was a clean distribution center. You can tell the centers that the employees have pride in. In these distribution centers when a worker sees trash on the floor, he/she goes out of their way to pick it up. Cleanliness also includes the location maintenance. How well are the storage locations maintained? Is there a worker responsible for each location?

Cleanliness and location maintenance ties to location accuracy. Location accuracy ties to inventory accuracy, which ties to customer fill rates and customer satisfaction. One tip for improving location cleanliness and maintenance is to assign a worker or team of workers to each aisle and put their name(s) on the end of the aisle and the location and inventory accuracy for the aisle. Not only will this build worker esteem and pride but it will build a little internal competition for the best accuracy rates.

**Time definite delivery.** Do you provide this to your customers? Do your suppliers provide it to you? Knowing when the deliveries will arrive (this may even be linked to advanced shipping notification) allows the distribution center manager to plan the work force around the delivery schedules. This planning ensures that the maximum work force is available to unload incoming deliveries and load outgoing deliveries. One center in Virginia that works with a major tobacco company not only knows exactly when to expect a delivery, it also knows if the truck is late based on its tracking systems and time definite delivery schedule.

**On-time deliveries.** This one ties to time definite deliveries but focuses on our deliveries to our customers. Are the trucks leaving our docks arriving to the customer as promised? Are we providing our customers with time definite deliveries? If our trucks are not arriving as promised do we know why? We had this problem at the National Training Center for a while. When we walked the process, we found that the times we expected the trucks and the delivery times the provided to the drivers were different.

**Logical warehouse/distribution center flow.** Do the supplies flow through your center in a logical manner? Most warehouses do not have a logical flow from receiving to storage locations or from receiving to customer staging locations or customer bins (if the customer picks up from the warehouse). Not having a logical flow of material through the warehouse results in additional "touches" or handling of the material more times than necessary. Additional handling can lead to lost or damaged items and contributes to additional waste of movement within the warehouse itself. The less an item moves in the warehouse the quicker it is where it is supposed to be and ready for issue.

**Employee education systems.** Toyota spent over fifty million dollars to develop the University of Toyota to educate its employees. Employees in their Ontario, California, Distribution Center are required to have eighty hours of training a year. That is a strong commitment to employee education. Technology in supply chain management has advanced rapidly over the past decade. If we do not keep our employees trained and up to date, how can we expect to compete with the companies that do such as Toyota? Employee education is not an option in today's business environment.

**Safety.** This is critical to retaining quality employees. If you do not provide your employees with a safe work environment, they will leave or worse, suffer a serious injury. If the employees do not feel safe, their productivity will suffer leading to a decrease in customer support and responsiveness. This will lead to a decrease in customers. A decrease in customers will eventually lead to the death of the company. This is the responsibility of leaders at all levels to ensure that workers feel safe in the work place.

**Layout.** The majority of a warehouse worker's time is traveling to a location to pick an order. Many of the warehouses and distribution centers that I have visited have the workers walking past locations of obsolete stocks to get to the locations of the active stocks. Fast moving stocks are scattered throughout the warehouse resulting in additional wasted movement for the workers. A good layout will place like ordered items close together, fast moving items closest to the customer locations or staging lanes, and in the ergonomic reach of the workers. Just as most warehouses use a form of ABC analysis for inventory frequency, warehouses and distribution centers could benefit from using an ABC analysis to identify fast moving items for locating closer to traffic areas.

**Obsolete Stocks.** While you are rewarehousing to get the fast movers closer to the customer area or traffic areas move the obsolete items out of the warehouse. What value do they add to your operation? More than a few managers have expressed concern over this comment because they "may need the item someday." If the item has not moved in a year, the chances are good that the item is of no value to you. If the item is of no value to you or your customer, it is costing you money in carrying costs to maintain it on your shelves.

**Turns.** When the Army started looking at inventory turns as part of the Velocity Management Program, the average number of turns for repair parts was less than three turns per year. Three turns per year is obviously not even close to world class. Dell on the other hand has at last reports more than sixty turns per year. That may be a bit too far to reach but anything less than twelve to fifteen turns per year may be an indicator that you are stocking either the wrong stuff or in the wrong quantity. You do not make money if the parts are not moving.

**Processing Times.** One major operation that I visited a couple of years ago was proud of the fact that they met their goals for dock to stock times. Our questioning of their goals revealed that their standards included three days to clear the dock and move the stocks to the functional areas of the warehouse and then three more days to have the stocks in the proper locations. This totals six days from truck to dock to stock. That is a lot of inventory that is not available for sale—not to mention that if the items are receipted but not on the shelf, you will never have good inventory accuracy. The standard for world class has to be clear the floor of today's work today regardless if it is in-processing the material or processing today's pick tickets today. Depending on the time buckets that your system measures, you should be able to apply a pit crew mentality to unloading a shipment and have it in the proper location in a matter of hours. World class distribution centers establish goals for orders picked per day per worker or per picking team.

**Cross Docking by Design—not by miracle.** For most distribution centers cross docking occurs as a miracle or because of a late shipment arriving just as the truck is ready to leave the dock. For world class centers cross docking is by design and areas are set aside for cross docking of important orders and critical materials. The first two weeks of operations of the Theater Distribution Center in Kuwait, the few cross docking operations were indeed a miracle even though the center was designed as a cross docking operation. After a few weeks of operations, the frequencies of cross docking improved because of careful attention to detail and leadership. Cross docking enables the distribution center personnel to handle items once as opposed to multiple times.

**Process Flow Charts.** World Class distribution centers have detailed process flow charts of the operations and post the charts for employee reference and guides. One of the requirements of ISO 9000 certification and competing for the Malcomb Baldridge Quality Award is a detailed process flow chart. Just as important as developing the chart is following and applying diagrams on the charts. Process flow charts serve multiple purposes. They enable workers to quickly refer to the charts if in question of what is the next action in the process and the charts serve as a great tool for educating new employees on the processes of the distribution center.

**Employee Involvement.** Getting employees involved in streamlining processes and solving problems is usually the best method of identifying problems and solutions. This is because the person doing the job is usually the subject matter expert in that particular process. Moreover, getting the employee involved in the solution gets the buy in of the employee as part of the solution and gets a stronger commitment to improving the process.

**Performance Based Standards.** The measures of effectiveness of a world class distribution center are performance based. More important the standards have to be perceived as achievable by the person being measured. Performance based measurements include orders picked per hour/day, shipments per worker per day, on time delivery, and the previously discussed perfect order fulfillment.

**Warehouse in a Warehouse Concept.** This attribute of world class distribution centers is a method of organizing the warehouse to reduce transit time in the distribution center or warehouse. The warehouse in a warehouse could be as simple as stocking all the parts for one particular model of equipment in one general area. The tool section at Lowe's and The Home Depot is an example of a warehouse in a warehouse. All of the tools are stored in one central location to control and consolidate the tools in the store. Stocking all of the service items in one location is another example of a warehouse in a warehouse. Using this concept improves response times to customers, reduces transit times in the warehouse, and contributes to improved inventory accuracy.

Can you be world class without meeting all of the above qualities? Yes, but the more of these qualities that you meet the harder it will be for your competition to creep up on you.

When working towards becoming a world class operation you have two choices. You can lead your company to world class or you can be like the dead fish. It is your choice. It takes a true leader to move an organization to world class.

# 9

## *Applying the Principles of War to Supply Chain Operations*

The military's principles of war date back to the Napoleonic Wars and the interpretation of Napoleon's strategy and tactics by Baron Henri Jomini and Karl Von Clausewitz. Their writings influenced modern writers such as J.F.C. Fuller and Liddell Hart. These principles are part of the instruction in almost every leadership course in the Department of Defense and the more senior courses delve into the writings of these authors in detail.

Field Manual 3-0, *Operations*, states: "The nine principles of war provide general guidance for conducting war and military operations other than war at the strategic, operational, and tactical levels. The principles are the enduring bedrock of Army doctrine. The US Army published its original principles after World War I. In the following years, the Army adjusted the original principles, but overall they have stood the tests of analysis, experimentation, and practice.

The principles of war are not a checklist. They do not apply in the same way to every situation."[1]

The Principles of War have not changed significantly over the past one hundred years and are:

1. **Mass**

2. **Offensive**

3. **Objective**

4. **Security**

---

1. *Field Manual 3-0, Operations*, US Army, 2001, paragraphs 4-33 and 4-34. FM 3-0 sets forth the Army doctrine for all Operations.

5.  **Simplicity**

6.  **Maneuver**

7.  **Unity of Command**

8.  **Surprise**

9.  **Economy of Force**

Let us look at each of these principles as they pertain to supply chain operations.

**Mass.** In military terms, this is the principle of placing as many forces as possible in action against an opponent. In supply chains, there is no difference. To be successful in supply chain operations, you have to put as many assets as possible against a problem area to prevent losing your clients or customers to a competitor. Although losing obviously has a much greater consequence in military operations, losing in supply chain operations can mean the end of the company.

**Offensive.** In successful military operations, you have to go on the offensive to defeat the enemy and take over his territory. In supply chains you have to be on the offensive to prevent losing business to a competitor. At the same time you have to be on the offensive to ensure that you are offering quality support, responsiveness, and value added services that your customers are demanding. Just as important you must do so before and better than the competition can.

**Objective.** Every military operation has an objective that must be secured or taken to meet the criteria of success for that operation. Imbedded in that objective is the center of gravity of the enemy. In a supply chain, operation there has to be an objective. In this context, the objective may be a new goal for customer support or customer wait times. The objective has to be clearly articulated and understood by all parties involved whether it is a military objective or a supply chain objective. Securing or meeting the objective is the measure of success of the operation.

**Security.** Security of supply chain operations has come to the forefront after the tragic September 11, 2001 attacks. Security of supply chains is necessary to prevent pilferage and loss of items in the supply chain. Security and visibility are the main reasons moving Radio Frequency Identification Technology to the forefront for supply chains.

A good example of security in military operations is the convoy operations in support of Operation Iraqi Freedom. Every supply convoy in support of the almost 250,000 soldiers and marines in Kuwait and Iraq started at the Theater Distribution Center in Kuwait. Security of these convoys was a necessary requirement to ensure the safety of the soldiers driving the trucks as well as the safety of the transported supplies. The only thing worse than losing valuable food, water, or ammunition was the loss of valuable soldiers to ambushes or other enemy attacks. Securing shipments from off shore suppliers is important and companies are becoming increasingly aware of the need to protect supplies and the supply chains. Sun Tzu told us twenty five hundred years ago that one of the quickest ways to victory was to attack the supply chains.

**Simplicity.** The best plan is usually the simplest plan. The simpler the plan the easier it is to understand by the people that have to implement it. There is no difference between the requirements for simple plans in commercial supply chains than the requirement for simplicity in military operational plans.

**Maneuver.** In military terms, this is the ability to move on the battlefield to gain an advantage over the enemy. In commercial supply chains, this is the ability to move on the business battlefield, provide goods and services quicker and better than a competitor can. Sometimes in the supply chain business, we have the opportunity to use a third party provider to maneuver for us when maneuver is not a core competency of the company.

**Unity of command.** This is critical to accomplishing objectives. Too many leaders and not enough followers create confusion and work in not completed. In supply chains, there is no difference. There has to be a single point of contact for customers for supply chain operations. Too many points of contact for customers create confusion among the customers. Too many chiefs in the warehouse create confusion on the warehouse floor. There has to be one leader for every organization and all of the subordinate sections have to be subordinate to that leader. In the military and in a supply chain unity of command is critical for success and achieving world class levels.

**Surprise.** Surprise is critical to success in military operations. Keeping the enemy in the dark on the plans for operations is critical to catching him/her off-guard and contributes to victory. Supply chain surprise may be as simple as being the first to market or the first to support a customer before the competition knows you have the capability to provide the service.

**Economy of force.** In military terms, this is using no more force than necessary to achieve an objective. In supply chains using more than the necessary resources will detract from the bottom line. In most warehouses, that I have been in no one has ever claimed to have too many workers so economy of force is also getting the most out of the workers that we do have.

Granted in supply chain operations the risks are not the life or death of our customers like the risks in the military. However, the success and life of our organization depends on the ability to use the same principles of war in supply chain operations as the military does for planning and conducting military operations.

# 10

## *Reverse Logistics*

*"In an ideal world, reverse logistics would not exist"*[1]

*Although this chapter does not directly related to Operation Iraqi Freedom, the impact of retrograding supplies, personnel, and equipment from the Iraqi Theater of Operations is a major concern for the Department of Defense. This chapter is an update of a previous work published in 2001. Recent studies reveal the cost of handling returns is as high as $150 per item returned.*[2] *Items ordered, but not really needed, before the start of Operation Iraqi Freedom and during combat operations fall into this category of returns. General Patton once said, "In battle, troops get temperamental and ask for things that they really do not need. However, where humanly possible, their requests, no matter how unreasonable should be answered." This is as true today as it was sixty years ago. However, the effort of the logisticians to supply the requested items of the soldiers results in excess and unneeded items in the theater. The resultant need to ship items back through the reverse pipeline is what prompted me to add this updated chapter.*

The problems associated with handling the return of unwanted or defective items by consumers have existed for years and the management and disposition of excess items has been a problem for retailers since the beginning of retail merchandising. According to Buzzy Wyland, the president of manufacturing services for GENCO Distribution Systems, reverse logistics operations was the last thing

---

1.  Jim Whalen, "In Through the Out Door," *Warehousing Management*, March 2001, p. 33.
2.  Mike Mannella, "What Your Returns Are Telling You," *APICS—The Performance Advantage*, July/August 2003, p.38.

that companies wanted to focus on.[3] The simple solution to reverse logistics was to pick up the damage or obsolete items from the vendor and discard them into a landfill. Estee Lauder Companies, Inc. dumped as much as $60 million in inventory into landfills annually before adopting a focus on the reverse supply chain.[4] Major corporations are discovering that focusing on reverse supply chain management is critical to profitability, supply availability, and improved customer responsiveness.

Ignoring the reverse supply chain is not a problem that is unique to the military. Commercial retailers historically experience a return of goods equivalent to between five and seven percent of total sales.[5] However, depending on the industry, the rate of returns can be as high as fifty percent (magazine publishing) and as low as two percent of sales (mail order computer manufacturers).[6] The rate of returned merchandise for most retailers becomes a bit skewed around the Christmas holiday period. Internet retailers experience return rates as high as twenty to fifty percent of sales.[7] One prominent Internet retailer, Amazon.com, claims to have less than one percent of total sales returned by their customers.[8] Another prominent mail order outdoor supplier has close to ten percent in returns. This return rate is much lower that the industry average. This company believes that the training of its employees is responsible for its low return rates.

The US Army experiences returned merchandise rates for serviceable supplies in excess of twenty percent of total requisitions.[9] These return rates rival those of some Internet retailers whose return rates also include the return of merchandise damaged in shipment. Commercial returns represent lost sales and lost profits. For every serviceable part in the reverse supply chain, there is a good possibility of another requirement for the same critical part by another customer. A serviceable part going backwards through the supply chain is not available, or visible, to the customer and in some cases the corporation.

3.    Whalen, "In Through the Out Door," p. 33.
4.    "Reverse Logistics," Informationweek.com, April 12, 1999.
5.    WERC Conference proceedings, 2000.
6.    Dale Rogers, *Going Backwards: Reverse Logistics Trends and Practices,* University of Nevada, Reno, NV, p. 7.
7.    WERC Conference proceedings, 2000.
8.    Conversation with Director of Logistics, Amazon.com, April 2000.
9.    Presentation to the Velocity Group Board of Directors, September 2000.

Commercial industry is moving towards complete outsourcing of customer returns. K-Mart uses a third party logistics provider[10] to process and prepare for resale its entire customer returned merchandise and the disposition of all excess stocks.[11] Until recently, Wal-Mart processed its own returns through one centralized distribution center solely for processing returned merchandise.[12] Studies of reverse supply chain-processing shows that it takes longer to process and restock returned merchandise than it does to process new material into the distribution center.[13] When electronic items are involved, an additional incurred cost is the cost to test the items before returning them to the shelf. Another cost to processing electronic items is the cost of obsolescence between the sale of the item, the return date, and the date the item is ready for resale.

Reverse supply chain management in commercial retail industry represents approximately $62 billion a year. Forrester Research in Cambridge, MA estimates that online purchased merchandise returns will exceed $11 billion dollars by 2002.[14] This represents a potentially huge problem for the commercial sector. Dr. Richard Dawe of the Fritz Institute of Logistics identifies six symptoms that indicate that there may be problems in the reverse supply chain.[15]

1. Returned merchandise or supplies arrive faster than they are processed or disposed of.

2. There are large amounts of returned inventory held in the distribution center or warehouse.

3. There are unidentified or unauthorized returns.

4. There is a lengthy processing cycle time for returned goods.

---

10. A Third Party Logistics provider is a company that specializes solely in logistics or supply chain operations as a core competency and thus provides a more cost efficient operation to its customers and frees the supported company from the burdens of internal logistics support.
11. Presentation by and discussions with the Ed Winter, Director of Reverse Supply Chain, K-Mart Corporation at the World Logistics Congress, March 16, 2001.
12. Tour of Wal-Mart facilities 1998.
13. Rogers, *Going Backwards,* p.39-40.
14. "Return to Sender," *Modern Materials Handling Magazine,* May 15, 2000, www.mmh.com
15. Beth Schwartz, "Reverse Logistics Strengthens Supply Chains," *Transportation and Distribution Magazine,* http://tdmagazine.com/FrmNewsLoader/index.asp?articleID=22157

5. The total cost of the returns process is unknown.

6. Customers lose confidence in the repair activities.

Each of these symptoms of a reverse supply chain problem represents areas that have the potential to reduce the efficiency of a distribution center or whole-sale depot. Reducing the efficiency of the military's wholesale depots results in longer customer wait times for critical repair parts and supplies. Longer wait times result in decreased operational readiness.

*"Now, more than ever, reverse logistics is seen as being important."*

—*Dale Rogers*[16]

In the introduction to *Going Backwards*, the first study on reverse logistics, the author states, "Reverse logistics is a new and emerging area, and as such, only a limited amount of information has been published to date."[17] Before the mid 1990s, the commercial firms with the most experience in managing returns through a reverse pipeline were catalog retailers. One early example of the impor-tance of an effective reverse supply chain is the expeditious manner that Johnson & Johnson dealt with the Tylenol tampering scare in the early 1980s. Dealing with returns is not a new phenomenon. However, it has received more attention in the last several years because of the Internet commerce explosion. This new interest has resulted in comprehensive studies by the Council of Logistics Man-agement and The University of Nevada, Reno and smaller studies by various firms that have been presented at various logistics conferences in the past several years.

The new focus on managing the reverse supply chain has it roots in the Euro-pean Union, specifically in Germany. Original concerns that prompted concen-trating on the reverse logistics processes were environmental. In 1991, Germany passed an ordinance that put teeth into the environmentally driven reverse supply chain. Strict environmental laws in Europe make the shipper responsible for dis-position of hazardous waste and recyclable materials. It did not take long before shippers started to realize that careful planning of the shipping of hazardous and recyclable items back to the distribution centers had positive impacts on the bot-tom line profits. Word quickly spread throughout the distribution community that managing the reverse supply chain could produce profits.

---

16. Rogers, *Going Backwards*, p.186
17. Ibid., page xiv.

Environmental concerns in Europe spread to the United States in the mid 1990s as more and more landfills became restrictive on the types of items that could be placed in the landfills. Manufacturers and distributors were forced to start planning ways to reclaim hazardous materials such as motor oils, automotive batteries, and tires to prevent paying environmental impact fees. The narrow focus on reclaiming and recycling hazardous materials led to companies looking at other initiatives to recapture some of the costs associated with managing the reverse supply chain.

Catalogers such as Lillian Vernon and L.L. Bean have dealt with the problem of processing returned merchandise since the beginning their operations.[18] Traditional retailers such as Sears and J.C. Penney solved the returns problem early on by allowing customers to return products ordered through the catalog to the retail stores for credit or exchange. Strictly dot.com companies do not have this luxury. Some of the more prominent "bricks and mortar" retailers, such as Borders, that also have Internet sales sites, have adopted a model that allows the return of items ordered over the Internet to the retail stores.[19] Best Buy recently adopted a similar policy of allowing Internet customers to return defective or unwanted items to their local retail stores. This policy, in the name of customer service, has the potential to create inventory problems at the retail stores, especially if the item is not a fast moving item. Items that are not normally stocked at the retail store or are slow moving items may very well find themselves in the reverse supply chain from the retail store back to the firm's distribution center or returns management center.

A study conducted by the University of Nevada, Reno in 1998 brought to light the magnitude of the financial impacts on companies by not managing the reverse supply chain. One of the participants in the study was K-Mart. K-Mart, like Wal-Mart and The Home Depot, has a very liberal customer returns policy. Although this liberal return policy is important in developing customer loyalty, it comes at a price. One of the costs of liberal returns is potential customer abuse of the system. K-Mart and The Home Depot have implemented centralized databases to track customer returns and identify potential abuses of the system.

Overwhelmed by the volume of returns in the reverse supply chain and the resultant drain on profitability, K-Mart turned to GENCO Distribution Systems to serve as the contracted operator of the reverse supply chain for all of their

---

18.   Arthur Schleifer, "L.L. Bean, Inc., Class Notes," Harvard Business School, Boston, MA. 1993.
19.   Borders presentation at WERC Conference, 2000

returned merchandise. Approximately two thirds of the items in their reverse supply chain are serviceable merchandise. The costs of processing the items in the reverse supply chain, above the costs of the items themselves, include:

1.   Merchandise credits to the customers.

2.   The transportation costs of moving the items from the retail stores to the central returns distribution center.

3.   The repackaging of the serviceable items for resale.

4.   The cost of warehousing the items awaiting disposition.

5.   The cost of disposing of items that is unserviceable, damaged, or obsolete.

6.   Fraud investigations.

7.   The manning of the service desk to receive items back from customers.

The return of serviceable items to the store shelves or to consumers through a secondary market such as flea markets, overseas sales, online auctions, and contributions to charitable organizations helps to offset portions of these costs. Contributions to charitable organizations such as Second Harvest do not return monies to the company but do provide tax deductions that contribute to the company's bottom line profits as well as providing "good will" for the corporation.

One major firm has managed to expand their reverse supply chain operations expertise into a company with over 4500 employees that operate out of eighty-five distribution centers worldwide, thirty five of these centers focus solely on reverse supply chain management. These distribution centers process approximately three to four billion dollars in returns for their customers each year.

Before contracting out the management of the reverse supply chain, Cheesebrough-Pond discarded or destroyed the majority of items returned to their six distribution centers.[20] The first year Cheesebrough-Ponds contracted out their reverse supply chain management resulted in an increase of over one million dollars profit through a combination of reduced destruction/land fill costs and the resale of products in lieu of destruction.

---

20.   Tom Andel, "Reverse Logistics: A Second Chance to Profit," *Transportation and Distribution Magazine,* July 1997.

BMG Music, like Cheesebrough-Ponds, uses automatic data collection to process returns into the distribution center. BMG, a large mail order music club, processes as many as 80,000 returned packages a day and averages close to 40,000 returned packages daily.[21] For BMG this represents approximately twenty percent of all packages shipped. BMG developed an automatic data collection system that allows them to use the same bar codes for processing returns as used for shipping the product to the customer. The use of the bar codes enables BMG to identify what customer account receives the credit and where in the distribution center the product is stored based on sales of the product.

Corporate interest in focusing core competencies is creating a trend in commercial industry to move away from the BMG model of handling returns in house and toward adopting the GENCO/K-Mart model of outsourcing the reverse supply chain and returned merchandise management. This outsourcing usually takes place in a centralized returns distribution center. The centralized system allows retail customers to return an item to the central distribution center that specializes in processing items in the reverse supply chain. The value of these centralized centers is that it allows companies to focus their efforts on the forward supply chain and allow the contracted company to focus on the items in the reverse supply chain.

Figure 6 shows the reverse supply chain and the accompanying decisions on the serviceability of an item. Figure 7 depicts the normal receipt processing at a distribution center. From two simple diagrams it is easy to see that processing items through the reverse supply chain are more complicated and time consuming that processing routine receipts at the distribution center or warehouse.

---

21. Clyde E. Witt, "Reverse Logistics at BMG," Supply Chain Flow Supplement to *Transportation and Distribution Magazine,* August 1998.

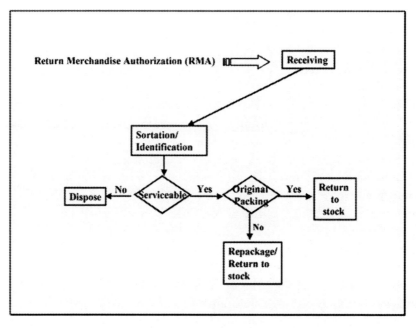

Figure 6. The Reverse Supply Chain Decisions and Actions

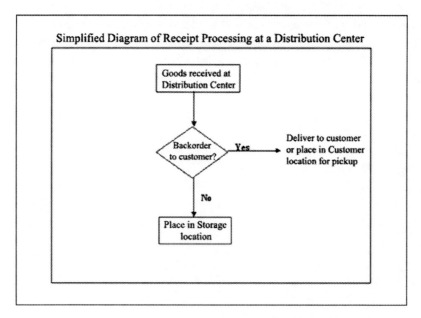

Figure 7. Simplified Receipt Processing for Routine Receipts at a Distribution Center for the Forward Supply Chain

In the automotive parts industry, the use of the reverse supply chain started during World War II, because of a shortage of parts. The remanufacturing and rebuilding of automotive parts is now a $36 billion dollar industry.[22] Between ninety and ninety-five percent of all starters and alternators sold in the US are remanufactured. [23] Volumes of these proportions require detailed and accurate information systems to support them. The use of a centralized returns center provides greater control using an automated system designed solely for reverse supply chain management.

The remanufacturing business for copier toner cartridges is now a billion-dollar business.[24] Hewlett-Packard goes as far as including a prepaid returns label in every cartridge and user replaceable printer part that they sell. This label contains a bar code to ensure proper return credit to the appropriate customer and for quick identification of the part in the shipping box.

This chapter has provided a snapshot of the practice of reverse supply chain management and its impacts in commercial industry. Although the focus on reverse supply chain management is relatively new, some segments of the commercial sector have been practicing reverse supply chain management for many years.

> *"The truth is, for one reason or another, materials do come back and it is up to those involved in the warehouse to effectively recover as much of the cost for these items as possible."*[25]

The problem of how to manage items in the reverse supply chain has existed for years. Catalog retailers have wrestled with this problem since the advent of catalog merchandising. Catalogers such as J.C. Penney and Sears are able to counter the problem by accepting merchandise back into their retail stores even if purchased through their catalog division. Other retailers and more recently e-tailers (merchants that sell exclusively through the Internet) have been forced to address the handling of returned merchandise rapidly to ensure proper credits are given to consumers. Another concern is getting the serviceable merchandise back on the shelves for resale.

---

22. Bruce Caldwell, "Reverse Logistics," Informationweek.com, April 12, 1999, http://www.informationweek.com/729/logistics.htm
23. Schwartz, "Reverse Logistics Strengthens Supply Chains," May 2, 2000, http://www.tdmagazine.com/FrmNewsLoader/index.asp?articleID=2215
24. Rogers, *Going Backwards*, page 173
25. Whalen, "In Through the Out Door," p. 33.

The key to the reverse logistics process is to determine why items are coming back through the system and then implement process improvement programs to prevent those reasons from occurring.

# 11

## *Conclusions, Lessons Learned, and the Applications of These Lessons to Your Supply Chain*

While there will always be a place for managers in the supply chain, leadership separates great organizations from good organizations. The greatest lesson from Operation Iraqi Freedom is that leadership makes the difference. Not all employees and managers react to stress in the same way. Leadership is the key to assisting your employees in getting through stressful times and situations.

Remember, leadership success depends on the people and not on processes. A great number of supply chain experts continue to focus on the management aspect of business. Your people are your greatest asset and they need leadership. Management should be reserved for processes and resources. Lead the people and manage the processes and you will create a world class supply chain or organization.

Throughout time, there has been a plethora of theories on management. The most prominent include Theory X, Theory Y, autocratic management, democratic management, and management by walking around. As Fran Tarkenton stated in the quote that started Chapter 2, "Leadership has to be demonstrated." Often in the Army, as in commercial business, we focus on accomplishing the mission or meeting the goals for the month or quarter and forget about the people. Regardless of what industry you work in you are in the people business.

When it comes to professional development, you are responsible for your own personal development. Seek improvement and do not wait for someone to provide it for you. The Army used to have the marketing slogan "Be all that you can be." If you are not being all that you can be because of personal professional development shortfalls do not blame it on someone else. Join a professional organization, take professional development classes, read books on your profession, and find a mentor to guide you.

Leaders have to be flexible and realize that there is no one size fits all style of leadership. Situations and personnel may dictate altering your style to meet the needs of the led.

Missions have to be clearly stated, clearly articulated, and most important of all clearly understood by the folks that have to make the mission happen.

Never sacrifice your family for the job. Remember the lines of the country music song a few years ago—no tombstone every had the words "if only I had spent more time at work." All too often, accomplishing the mission comes at the expense of a leader's family. You have to find a balance. You can never replace the time away from your family while they are growing up.

It is amazing how people handle and react to stress. More than a few folks reacted poorly to the stress of wartime operations. The best example I can provide of leaders not handling stress is of a general officer on March 26, 2003 (day six of hostilities). On that particular day, we arrived back from the Theater Distribution Center to Camp Arifjan about seven thirty in the evening (just enough time to get to the dining facility before it closed). As we sat down to dinner, the Scud alarm went off. This was not good timing from my perspective. As all the soldiers in the dining facility quickly stopped eating and donned their protective masks, one general officer started running through the dining facility calling the soldiers names for not moving to the outside walls quick enough. Most of the soldiers were taking the time to put on their protective suits. The irony of this general making a fool out of himself was that he was the only person in the facility that was not wearing a protective mask. Had a Scud indeed landed near by, he would have been the only one not protected against a chemical or biological attack. It is important for leaders to set the example and assist their employees in handling stress. The handling of stress is a little like the old deodorant commercial, "Never let them see you sweat." Leaders have to harness the power of stress to lead effectively. Stress is inherent in daily life. Harness the power of stress. Also of importance is do not create additional stress on your employees because of your inability to effectively handle stress.

Communications and knowing the importance of your job are the keys to success in any operation. Once the soldiers working in the Theater Distribution Center understood the criticality of their mission and their role in the overall operation, getting supplies processed and moved was much easier. Your communications have to be clear and concise. If your employees do not completely understand your guidance, you are not communicating.

You have to be on the ground to see what is really happening. Too many folks are content to sit behind a desk and make assumptions about what is going on in the field. This is not unique to the Army. Look around your company and you will see the same thing. Managers can manage from the data on the computer screens and printouts but leaders have to be out of the office and personally observing the operations to effectively lead.

The power of leadership is amazing. With the right leaders in the right positions, anything is possible and achievable in any organization. The workers just want someone to talk to them, ask them what they are doing, provide direction, and show genuine concern about the job and the working conditions.

Never lose focus of the mission at hand. All too often, it is easy to lose focus of what is important. During Operation Iraqi Freedom, the most important mission was the welfare of the soldier. Too many people were running around more concerned with the hours they worked or their personal conditions rather than focusing on taking care of the soldiers. In business, it is the same thing. Too many people are concerned with what is best for them and their careers and not what is best for the employees. It is a win-win situation. Take care of the employees and your career will advance itself.

Do not get personally tied to an idea. Conversely, do not act as if an idea has no merit just because you did not think of it. No one has a lock on all of the good ideas. At the same time, do not ask your subordinates for their input or opinions of your ideas if you really do not want to hear them. How often has someone asked for your input or comments and then chastised you publicly for speaking up? Encourage candor in your subordinates and accept their responses without retribution.

What have you done for your customer lately? In the late 1980s, Janet Jackson had a song that asked the question, "What have you done for me lately?" You should be able to answer that question for your customers. In fact, if your customers have to ask that question, you have a problem. Regardless of how well you think you did in supporting the customer, it is their perception that really answers the question. If the customer does not feel that you took care of them, then you have a real problem and may lose that customer.

Leaders have to have a passion for the work they are doing and the people they have working for them. If you lose this passion for either the work or the people, it is time for you to move on before you cause detriment to your organization.

Supply chain planning is every bit as important as operational planning. There is a close link between these areas. If you focus only on the operations without the proper focus on the supply chain, you will have problems. Consequently, if you cannot support an operational plan, speak up before someone gets hurt.

Remain flexible. A plan may have to change as soon as operations start. Be prepared for the change and be ready to react.

Do not point fingers of blame. Identify the problem and get it in the right channels to get it fixed. Leaders solve problems. Do not just talk about them or complain about them. You have to be part of the solution. If you present a problem to your boss, be ready to recommend a solution to fix it. Remember, everyone's perspective is based on where they are and what they are tasked to do. Try to get the entire picture and work on a joint solution.

Always be completely honest with your employees. Once you compromise your integrity, they will always question your motives and your every statement.

Mentor and develop your subordinates. They are your legacy to the company. When you mentor them, be honest about their strengths and weaknesses. If a subordinate has a shortcoming, tell him/her. Then, give them guidance on how to improve their performance.

Always remember—regardless of what business you think you are in, you are in the people business! If you are not taking care of your employees, you are in the wrong line of work.

I sincerely hope that you found ideas in the book that you can apply to your operations. You can reach me at joewalden@aol.com if this book has prompted any questions or topics of discussion.

# *Logistics team gets VP's 'Golden Hammer'*

*by Gerry J. Gilmore*

WASHINGTON (Army News Service, June 11, 1998)—A group of logisticians at Fort Lee, Va., will receive a prestigious executive branch award June 12 for their successful efforts in streamlining the Army's supply process.

The logisticians earned Vice President Al Gore's "Golden Hammer" award. Established in 1993, the "Golden Hammer" recognizes teams of federal, state or local government employees for their efforts in reducing bureaucracy, putting customers first, empowering employees and simplifying governmental processes. More than 1,000 "Hammer" awards have been presented since the program's inception.

The Fort Lee recipients—current and former military and civilian logisticians—put together the Army's new supply, maintenance and financial process called velocity management. It is a process improvement program based on best-business practices, said Quartermaster Corps Lt. Col. Joe Walden, who heads the Velocity Management Team, part of Fort Lee's U.S. Army Combined Arms Support Command.

Walden said velocity management initiatives, a key component in future Army operational strategy, have enabled the Army to save more than $75 million during the past two years and forecast projected savings of $30 million this fiscal year.

Other velocity management team members include Lt. Col. John Simpson, Maj. Gus Pagonis, Chief Warrant Officer (CW5) Leo Gibson, Chief Warrant Officer (CW3) Gene Perrino, Mrs. Jan Smith, Harry Johnson (contractor), Lowell Lovin, (contractor) and Bruce Hackett (contractor).

The CASCOM and Fort Lee commander, Maj. Gen. Dan Brown, will present the award on behalf of the National Partnership for Reinventing Government. Several former team members will also be present at the ceremony, to be held at CASCOM headquarters.

"Velocity management is applicable in garrison and deployment [environ-ments]," Walden said. "The aim of velocity management is to get support to the soldier as quickly and efficiently as any first-rate commercial firm, while still pro-viding a hedge against unforeseen interruptions in the logistics cycle."

The Army is adopting velocity management logistics to save time and money, Walden said. The system cuts out the "middleman," or unwieldy large warehous-ing operations and their attendant costs, he said. Advances in computer technol-ogy and telecommunications now enable the shipment of parts and supplies straight from the manufacturer to the customer.

Shipments can also be tracked en route, allowing flexible deliveries to custom-ers, Walden said. Tank parts needed for repairs in the field, for example, can be diverted in case the customer, such as a mobile armored division, moves on to another location.

Velocity management efforts have enabled the Army to decrease its average repair cycle times (deadline, or unusable to mission-capable equipment) by 35 percent during the past two years, Walden said.

"The goal of velocity management is to improve readiness while reducing costs and improving logistics responsiveness," he said.

The Army's Velocity Management Program started in 1995 after a study by the RAND Corporation on streamlining logistics, Walden said. The CASCOM commander was appointed as the Executive Agent for Velocity Management by the Department of the Army's Deputy Chief of Staff for Logistics. A team was established within CASCOM to implement the program Armywide.

The program is managed through the use of four Process Improvement Teams, Walden said. These teams are focused on repair cycle time reductions, order-ship time reductions, stockage determination—developing the optimal stockage policy and financial/logistical interfaces, he said.

The CASCOM Velocity Management Team works the day-to-day manage-ment of these teams, which have conducted walk-through assistance visits at every Army installation with the exception of those in Alaska, and that is sched-uled for June 15-19, Walden said.

The efforts of the CASCOM team under the guidance of Tom Edwards, dep-uty to the CASCOM commander, Walden said, have produced a 50-percent reduction in the order-ship times across the Army and a 55-percent reduction in the order-ship times for the Army's most-deployable Forces Command units.

# Suggested Readings and Sources of Information

1. Thompson, Julian, *Lifeblood of War—Logistics in Armed Conflict*, Marston Book Services, Abingdon, England, 1991.

2. Collins, Jim, *Good to Great*, HarperCollins Publishers, New York, 2001.

3. Appleman, R.E., *South to the Naktong, North to the Yalu/The United States in the Korean War*, Office of the Chief of Military History, Department of the Army, Washington, DC, 1961.

4. Blanchard, Ken and Peale, Norman Vincent, *The Power of Ethical Management*, Ballantine Books, New York, 1988.

5. Ridge, Warren J., *Follow Me*, 1989, AMACOM, NY.

6. Wright, K.R., *The Few The Proud The Bankrupt*, Biddle Publishing Company, Brunswick, ME, 2000.

7. Sandras, William A., Jr., *Just-in-Time: Making it Happen*, Oliver Wight Publications, Essex, VT, 1989

8. Goldratt, Elihu, *The Theory of Constraints*, The North River Press Publishing Corporation, Great Barrington, MA, 1990.

9. Rogers, Dale, Going *Backwards: Reverse Logistics Trends and Practices,* University of Nevada, Reno.

10. Napolitano, Maida, *Making the Move to Cross Docking*, Warehousing Education and Research Council, Oak Brook, IL, 2000.

11. Peters, Tom, and Waterman, Robert H., Jr., *In Search of Excellence,* HarperCollins Publishers, New York, 1982.

12. Tompkins, James A., *No Boundaries,* Tompkins Press, Raleigh, NC, 2000.

13. Marcus, Bernie, and Blank, Arthur, *Built From Scratch,* Times Books, New York, 1999.

14. Pande, Peter, et al, *The Six Sigma Way,* McGraw Hill, New York, 2000.

15. Johnson, Spencer, *Who Moved My Cheese?,* G.P. Putnam's Sons, New York, 1998.

16. Sun Tzu, *The Art of War,* translated by Ralph D. Sawyer, Barnes and Noble, 1994.

17. Musashi, Miyamoto, *The Book of Five Rings,* Bantam Books, New York, 1982.

Professional Organizations:

1. Warehousing Education and Research Council, **http://www.werc.org**. WERC is a great source of information on distribution and produces an e-mail newsletter.

2. APICS—the Education Society for Resource Management, **http://www.apics.org**. APICS was originally formed as the American Production and Inventory Control Society. APICS sponsors the distribution and production industry standard for certification through its CPIM, CFPIM, and CIRM programs.

3. Council of Logistics Management, **http://www.clm1.org**.

4. Material Handling Management Society, **http://www.mhms.org**.

# BIOGRAPHY—COL Joseph L Walden

Joe Walden has over twenty-five years of supply chain and leadership experience.

He was commissioned a Quartermaster Officer after graduating from North Carolina State University in 1978 with a degree in Rural Sociology. He served as an Assistant Adjutant (personnel officer), Main Supply Platoon Leader, and Supply Control Officer in the 25th Supply and Transport Battalion, Schofield Barracks, Hawaii, from 1978 to 1982. He then served as the Installation Supply Officer, Signal Brigade S4 (Logistics Officer), and a Signal Company Commander at Fort Gordon, Georgia, from 1982 to 1986. After command, COL Walden attended graduate school from 1986 to 1988 at Florida Institute of Technology in Melbourne, Florida. Upon completion of graduate school, he was assigned to the Directorate of Combat Developments at the Quartermaster School, Fort Lee, Virginia, where he was a Logistics Plans Officer and the Chief of the General Support Branch from 1988 to 1991. He was assigned to the 3rd Corps Support Command in Wiesbaden, Germany, from 1992 to 1995. During this time Joe was the Executive Officer of the 19th Corps Materiel Management Center and Chief of the Supply Management Division within the Corps Support Command's Support Operations Directorate. In 1995, Joe moved to Fort Irwin, California, where assumed command as the first commander of the National

Training Center Materiel Management Center (a distribution management battalion). After changing command in 1997, he was assigned to the Combined Arms Support Command at Fort Lee, Virginia. He was dual hatted as the Chief of the Velocity Management Program and Chief of the Concepts and Doctrine Division for Combat Developments. In 1999, he was assigned to the School of Advanced Military Studies, Fort Leavenworth, Kansas, as a student in the Advanced Operational Art Studies Fellowship and then as the Chief of the *FM 3-0, Operations*, Doctrine Writing Team. On June 13, 2003, Joe returned to Fort Irwin and became the third Commander of the National Training Center Theater Support Command. During his command tour, COL Walden was selected by name to establish the Theater Distribution Center and serve as Director of the 377th Distribution Management Center in support of Operation Iraqi Freedom, Camp Arifjan, Kuwait.

He is currently the Director of the Army's School for Command Preparation at Fort Leavenworth, Kansas.

His military schooling includes the Quartermaster Officer Basic and Advanced Courses, the Army Command and General Staff College, the US Air Force Air Command and Staff College, the Defense Strategy Course, the US Air Force Air War College and the Senior Service College Advanced Operational Art Studies Fellowship.

His civilian education includes a Bachelor of Science in Rural Sociology from North Carolina State University, an MBA with a concentration in Logistics Management and an MS in Systems Management from Florida Institute of Technology, and a Masters of Military Arts and Sciences in Theater Operations from the US Army Command and General Staff College.

In addition, he is one of only a few soldiers Certified in Production and Inventory Management (CPIM) by APICS and was recently recognized with the prestigious Certified Fellow in Production and Inventory Management (CFPIM). COL Walden serves as a member of the Warehousing Education and Research Council's Education Committee and is a member of the Material Handling Management Society.

Colonel Walden has published monographs on Just-in-Time Logistics and Reverse Logistics, co-authored a handbook on warehousing operations for the Army, and edited a textbook on Logistics Planning. He has published numerous articles for leading supply chain magazines and made over one hundred presentations to professional organizations and colleges on Supply Chain Management issues and solutions.

In 2002 he was selected one of the "Up and Coming Logistics Executives in America." He was recently selected as one of the "Top 20 Logistics Executives in America for 2003" by the International Logistics Forum. He has been profiled in "Who's Who in America" for the past decade and has been profiled in "Who's Who in the World."

COL Walden is married to the former Kay Johnson of Westphalia, Kansas and they have two daughters, Amber and Bobbi.

0-595-29496-0

Printed in the United States
79963LV00005B/52-78